To Claire

We were so than
feet done which.
meet on 10th March 2011
May you find my life story
interesting + increase your faith
Best wishes
Josephine

# BLESSINGS
# AND
# TESTINGS

A Twentieth Century
Christian Life

By Josephine E. Bagby

*AuthorHouse™ UK Ltd.*
*500 Avebury Boulevard*
*Central Milton Keynes, MK9 2BE*
*www.authorhouse.co.uk*
*Phone: 08001974150*

*First published by AuthorHouse 11/06/2009*

*978-1-4490-4984-3 (sc)*

*This book is printed on acid-free paper.*

# Dedication

## To the memory of Meryl Ralphs

Without Meryl Jesus might not have become my Lord forty-five years ago, I might never have started upon my journey of faith and this story would never have been told. She prayed for me, supported me, and invited me to *Lee Abbey* where I was born again. She later became Godmother to my daughter.

# Contents

# Acknowledgements

I should like to acknowledge the contribution of my sister, Diana, who took on the mammoth task of reading and studying my scribbled notes, and diaries, and assembling, editing, and typing them. God had nine times told me to write, but I had flunked out because I foresaw all the problems. Just as Moses needed Aaron, I knew I needed Diana.

I should like to thank Peter, her husband, for using his skills on my behalf. His knowledge of modern technology was invaluable in processing the typescript into a book.

As you read, many names crop up in the text. My thanks go to all these named friends and acquaintances, whose influence has blessed me in the course of my life. My prayer is that this book may be a blessing not only to them, but also to their families, to my family and to future generations.

# Preface

My prayer in writing this book is that you, my readers, may be led to realise that God has a new, far better, life prepared for you, just as he had for me. He asked me to bow down before him more than forty-five years ago. He may also be calling you to surrender to Jesus and make him your Lord and Saviour. Do, please, get in touch with other believers, spend time quietly with God each day, learn all you can about the Father, Son, and Holy Spirit, and depend upon them to guide you in the future. You too will be richly blessed, even when tested.

Josephine E. Bagby

## CHAPTER ONE: EARLY YEARS

It was on 6$^{th}$ December 1929, a month earlier than expected, that I came into the world. My parents, John and Dorothy Pheysey, a devoted couple, already had another daughter, Diana, one year and eight months old. Our father farmed the land opposite the Castle of the Bishop of Worcester in Hartlebury, and this is where we were raised. We were both christened at Hartlebury Parish Church, and I still have the prayer book the Rector gave for me when I was christened. My parents were regular church goers and my Father was for many years a Church Warden at Hartlebury and elsewhere. I remember being held by my Father's hand as we walked to church and also sitting through the Litany as well as Matins. So I was introduced to Christian worship at an early age. When I was three, my Father and his cousin's husband, who was a carpenter, built a marvellous caravan. It was called "The Ark" for we all went in two-by-two: 2 parents, 2 children, 2 maids and 2 Old English sheep dogs called Meg and Rough. We had wonderful holidays at resorts such as Saundersfoot, Aberystwyth, Borth, and Barmouth.

One year my sister and I both had chickenpox, caught from the Bishop's daughter, and afterwards my parents thought it would be good to get us away to the seaside, even though it was December. At Weston-Super-Mare they took us into a farmer's yard for shelter from bad weather. The maid stepped from the caravan into the lean-to tent only to find she was up to her knees in water on which rubbish was floating. The dogs were swimming. This happened on the night of my 6$^{th}$ birthday. We two girls were carried on the shoulders of adults up to the farmhouse for safety. I remember it had only got oil lamps. Father was rushing to move the van before the water rose up to the door and wet the interior. My chief concern was for "Neddy", a donkey on wheels I had been given for my birthday, also for "Tishee", a horse that was on elastic so it could be pulled into different shapes.

These camping holidays were to start the liking for camping that was to come later in my life. I still have the board on which the plan for "The Ark" was drawn to scale. There was a double bed across the front. The door was on the near side just beyond the edge of this bed. Opposite the door was a sink with cupboards beneath, and then the wardrobe. On the right of the door was the paraffin stove which had

1

two burners whose wicks had to be cleaned. Next to the stove was a big grocery cupboard. When the doors of the wardrobe and grocery cupboard were opened they met, so as to close off the rear of the van which had a table at the rear end and the children's beds on each side. All bedding went into lockers beneath the beds which became seats during the day. Beneath the curved roof and at both ends of the van there were windows of various sizes. The van weighed 17 hundredweight and was pulled by a Morris car. Mother drove it as well as Father. I remember on one occasion she was driving and the van developed a swing and it touched a car that was being driven in the opposite direction. (They had not invented stabilizers in those days.) We had to go to a police station to report it. I thought Mother would go to prison, but no, the offence was not serious.

We used to have four tall aluminium water carriers that each held about six pints. Milk we got straight from the cow when milking time was over. Fees for camping were seven shillings and six pence (about 35p) a week compared with £8.50p or more today for one night.

We gave nicknames to the other campers. When we had been swimming in the sea and fishing in the rock pools we hung our swimming costumes out to dry on the tent ropes. Cows came round grazing and one day a cow's horn got through the strap of a bathing costume. She pulled it off the rope and went round with it hanging down over her face until we rescued it from her.

Borth was a wonderful place for thunderstorms. They echoed round the mountains and seemed to go round and come back again.

Dad would sometimes come down just at weekends. We would have a competition to see who would be first to spot his car.

The journey was 108 miles. To make the time go faster we watched from the car windows to see who could count the most Automobile Association men on their motor bikes or the most ice cream men with their "stop-me-and-buy-one" tricycles.

We had a picnic lunch somewhere on the way where there was a lay-by near a shallow river in which we could go and play.

Sometimes we had relatives who would bring their van and camp beside us. I remember going to Aberystwyth with them one year to see Deanna Durbin in "*A Hundred Men and a Girl*". We seemed to have warm summers and enjoyable times together.

We were camping at Borth when the Second World War broke out. Because of this we were going home early. I can now see the cars that stopped to hear the announcement that it was indeed true that war had started. Cars did not have radios fitted inside as today's cars do. Our radio was a big box-like thing that Dad put on the car roof to get a good reception. That's how others saw what we were doing and stopped to join the solemn party. We did not go camping again until after the war was over.

**Secondary School**

When I was ready for secondary school my parents chose a boarding school for me – Overstone, near Northampton. It was a school of the Parents' National Educational Union (PNEU). All exams were set at Ambleside. It was a school for those who found school work hard to learn, for all was done by repetition of lessons to put them into a thick head. Mother and I first went for an interview. We travelled by train from Birmingham to Northampton and took a taxi to the school. Miss Wix and Mrs Esslemont were the head teachers and I was asked by Mrs Esslemont what was my favourite subject. I quickly replied, "Oh, riding!" "I don't call that a subject", she said. They did have riding lessons at week-ends but they were too expensive for me to have them.

The interview was in war time and there was a black-out after dark. When we got back to Birmingham there was also a pea soup fog. We waited at the bus stop to go home from the station but no bus came. We could not see the notice that said that after 4.00 p.m. the bus left from a different stop and by the time we found this out the last bus had gone. Mother phoned relatives who lived in Carpenter's Road and we stayed the night with them. During the night there was an air raid and when Uncle Bill drove us in his car to get our bus home we saw a church completely flattened, but "The Lord's Prayer" written in big gold letters on a black background was left standing undamaged. I can see it now and it made a big impact on me at the time.

I was accepted by Overstone School and went there from 1943 – 1946. I have a set of postcards of the school and grounds and all my diaries of the time that I was there. I was put into Onyx House and we wore cloaks with the gem colours in the hood. Mine was black and white. Other Houses were: Garnet (red), Jasper (green) and Topaz (gold). New girls were put into the care of an older girl. (I had a Jewish girl who was horrid to me). The older girl was from the same form and dormitory and was supposed to help the younger to learn the ropes and find her way around, for the class rooms were converted stables some quarter of a mile away.

We did realise there was a war on at Overstone. The head let the senior school go to her room to listen to the radio for news of the D-Day landings. There were no television screens to watch then, only the *Pathé* news in the cinemas could show the pictures, or *Picture Post* magazine. Some of the pictures in that were too disturbing for children's eyes and we were not allowed to look at it.

Just before D-Day we also had the American Army soldiers camped in the park belonging to Overstone School. We used to see them across the lake and beyond the swimming pool out in the fields. We heard their bugles and their chatter. My dormitory prefect was in the cricket team and the netball team. These teams were allowed to meet and play against the Americans and we were all agog to hear what had taken place when she came to bed later than the rest of us. Over the nine terms the dormitories I had to sleep in were called: Tower, Wantage, Gate, Honesty, Tipperary, Blanket and Crow's Nest. I slept in some more than once.

My school diary gives details of speakers that came to the school. One I liked told us about his work at the BBC. In the year after the war we had coaches to take us to London to see the play "The Importance of being Ernest". How good it felt to be out of four walls! The capital city, though war torn and scarred, gave us great excitement.

At school we called the teachers "Ma'am" and were taught to speak "nicely". My sister said "Oh, you do sound Overstonish!" when I returned home for the holidays. It was while I was there that I was confirmed by the Bishop of Peterborough on March 4th 1945. We all had to attend classes beforehand. All I can remember about these classes today was that we had to repeat weekly, "Confirmation is an outward and visible sign of an inward and spiritual grace." My sister had been confirmed in Wales a week before my confirmation. Mother had made her a confirmation dress out of a parachute. Since clothes were rationed, she brought this dress for me too. Because we were different sizes I tried it on and Mother altered it in the hotel room she stayed in for the weekend. We had veils and white gloves, so different from today when jeans or a skirt are worn.

My father came one day to look at a farm in Moulton which was near my school. He thought he would call on the off chance of seeing me. I was so surprised to see him standing in the hall with his back to the fire place. We only had a few minutes together as it was not a parents' visiting weekend. (These weekends took place once or twice a term.)

I was dreadfully homesick and hated every minute, especially if I was ill and in sick bay all alone which happened about once a term. One term we had measles and three quarters of the school went down with it. Sick bay was not able to cope. Girls in dormitories nearest to sick bay were moved to empty beds in other dorms. I had already had measles, so I was the one that kept going to classes and other school activities. Father said, "You will never be any good unless you do your sums and other assignments". He returned my letters home with mistakes underlined and corrected.

In my last year at Overstone there were four or five of us who did not want to take the School Certificate examination. We were given a small classroom at the end of the music wing where people had their lessons and where they practised. We were allowed to do an extra subject, "housewifery". This was cooking in the small cottage which housed some of the teachers.

For our Geography lessons we had a choice of countries to study. I chose Holland as I had met a very nice Dutch sailor.

Leaving school was the happiest day of my life until then. As the coach left to take us to the station I said I would never go back there again.

After leaving school I went to Birmingham College of Domestic Science for a year's course on Housewifery, but I had only been going there for 3 weeks when I caught primary typical pneumonia and was very ill for a month or more with a temperature of 104 day in and day out. I was given M & B, the only drug available in those days before antibiotics were invented. It left a scar on my lung which is still there today. I had to wear a vest of some kind of material that kept me cosy and warm. Because I had missed so much of the college term I was advised to restart the same course the

5

following year. I never did go back because what happened next was that my mother had a severe heart attack and was told she must not carry so much as a handbag. She had been holding a ladder, with her arms raised, while cutting branches of a winter-flowering cherry tree to decorate the Church for Christmas. When she saw the decorations in the house she said, "Why are these decorations here? Is it Christmas?" A doctor was called who said she had had a heart attack.

So I was home help and farm worker instead of a domestic science student. I joined the Women's Institute and was a member for 16 years.

**The Women's Institute and Young Farmers Clubs**

As a member of the Women's Institute, I took examinations in *Cookery and Preservation* for demonstrator and judging purposes, six exams in all. Some foods were still rationed when I took the exams. I remember the cookery exam included doing a three-course meal for two people for 10/- (i.e. 50p). I did potato and parsley soup, followed by mixed grill of liver, sausage, bacon, watercress, tomato and angels-on-horseback. For dessert I made a biscuit and chocolate foundation with peaches and cream on top. We also had to make scones and pastry of some sort, all in front of judges. I passed with first class. The preservation exam required bottled fruit, jam, dried herbs and chutney, all prepared beforehand. Some bottling had to be done in front of the judges. I failed the dried herbs part of the test because I presented the herbs in jars whose lids still bore the name of Heinz or Colman. I had to do them all again. Having done the practical tests, I went on to the examination for judges, and spent many years thereafter judging cookery and preservation at W.I. shows and also for Young Farmers Clubs. I had joined the YFC after leaving school and had a lot of outings and experience in competitions with a nearby Branch. I made friends that lasted for years. Some of the boys became boy-friends and even asked me to marry them but I was not in love.

**Learning to drive**

My father taught me to drive a car in the farm fields and on our private drive before we went on the public highway. I was so nervous that I often ended up in tears, as he shouted at me, "Get on, you silly little girl! Of course you can do it!" I had said I would never overtake anything or do more than 30 miles an hour, and I had threatened never to sit behind a wheel again if I did not pass my driving test. I always got on my knees and prayed to God for help before driving anywhere! The test was on December 31$^{st}$ when it was cold and foggy. Mother drove me to the test station in Kidderminster. The first thing I had to do was start on a hill. Then a dog on heat, followed by other dogs ran across the road in front of me. The examiner said, "That's your emergency stop. I won't give you another one." Father had taught me to do a three-point turn using the clutch and the accelerator but not the brake. A friend had told me not to go slowly in a thirty-mile limit zone as she had been failed on this point. So I kept up to 30 miles per hour when it was possible to do so. We went the rounds and I was sure I had failed. However, when I had returned and parked, the examiner said, "Well, Miss Pheysey, you are inclined to go too fast and to follow the car in front at T junctions where you must stop even if the road is clear. You should use your brake, but what you did shows you have the ability to control the car. You have passed." I drove to where Mother was waiting and she drove home. My parents had driven cars before tests were introduced so they had not taken them themselves. For the first 14 years (including the learning period) I was using my father's cars. I had no idea then that later I would one day be driving a 19 foot caravan. It is 39 years since I have owned a car myself, though I have driven for 53 years. I know for certain that God has heard my prayers and put his angels in charge to protect me and save me from accidents.

**Early involvement in the Occult**

One thing that happened at Overstone School was that I met a girl there who was into things of the occult. She recognised I was "a natural" and encouraged me to do certain tricks with her, like willing people to turn round when standing in the dinner queue. Another trick was that we would each hold a hand of four or five cards and ask each other to pick out one of the cards with the words, "Think of a black velvet curtain and pull out the ace of spades". I was good at this in her opinion. She then told me about palmistry, reading the lines on the hand and telling me what they meant. One thing I did not understand was that she was always cutting herself on the back of her hands with a razor blade. This was the start of my interest in the occult. "The Old D", as I call the Devil, was after me in a big way and had his people all lined up to take me further into his clutches with increasing severity and with disastrous results

After I had left school, the pianist for a class where I went to learn ballroom dancing was also involved in the occult and told fortunes. She got me more interested in the subject and I read her books. This was another stage in the downhill process of my becoming involved in occult things. I found that I became popular at the Young Farmers Club, where my talent was in demand by young people who wanted to know their fortune.

Another step was taken in this direction when my mother's sister, May, came over from Canada to stay with us in 1947. Another sister of Mother's, Eva, came to stay at the same time. They had both been brought up with an interest in spirits. Their father, my grandfather, founded and paid for the Spiritualist Church to be started in Stourbridge. Aunty May and Aunty Eva told fortunes by reading teacups and Aunty Eva by automatic writing. These were gifts of the Devil, though at the time I did not know they were from him. I got more involved when I went over to Canada for five months from April to August 1956 to stay with Aunt May's daughter, and her family. I told fortunes to passengers and crew on the boat, *"The Empress of France"* and had queues waiting to have their fortunes told by palmistry. This disrupted the ship, and the bursar asked me to stop doing it.

I returned on the same ship and my Father's sister, Norah, came to meet me and to drive me home. We became very close, as she had lost her husband in 1947, when her children were between one and four years old and she had gone to séances to try to contact her husband. It was through her taking me to one or two séances while I was staying with her in Scotland that I became friends with mediums. I then went to the Spiritualist church in Stourbridge on a few occasions to see if I got anything from the Spirit World. I did, and so got more interested in it. I also discovered they did healing. I was then suffering from arthritis in my knees and was taking pain killers to keep going. Then one of my boyfriends, Alec, from the Young Farmers' Club was killed in a car accident. Someone fell asleep at the wheel and drove straight into his car. It happened in

Scotland. Now there was even more reason to go to my aunt's mediums in Scotland to see if he wanted to contact me. He did, and information was given me that no one else could possibly have known, such as greetings cards he had given me. One card said "Tulips and heather, tied up together, tell of my love for you." There was a song of the same words that was a hit at the time. There were also details of places we had visited, nicknames we had for each other, and different ways of pronouncing words such as "scone". He came from Aberdeen so he had a Scottish way of pronouncing words. All this from the medium convinced me it was Alec.

I had more words come through the medium about my grandfather who had died in 1961. The medium mentioned a bullock we had named Ferdinand, and explained why we had removed the climbing rose from the wall of my grandfather's house and put wisteria there instead, and why we had changed the way the front door had opened. This information was all true.

More involvement came when my father went very nearly blind with glaucoma. I wrote to the Spiritualist Healer, Harry Edwards, for healing to be sought for Father. If only the Anglican Church had had healing services, things might have been very different. There was a monthly prayer fellowship, but I always came away from that feeling very frustrated. For various reasons I got involved step by step in the occult until I was hooked.

The more I went into the occult, the lonelier and more depressed I became. Friends had got married and had their own families, and some were afraid of my psychic ability and cut off friendships when they knew about it. One man was a concerned Christian and went to his church for advice. He had invited me to go to his home, but I knew I would not be there for, in my sleep, I had been astral travelling. I had seen his home dining room and the table set and people sitting down at a meal, but I was not there. When I told him this he took his leave.

My parents saw me getting more and more withdrawn and unhappy and alone over a period of ten years.

**Born Again!**

Then God sent a born again Christian girl named Meryl Ralphs into the church choir at Broome. She was a couple of years younger than I was, but had a similar interest in cookery. She was a demonstrator of cookery and ovens for the Midlands Electricity Board at that time.

(She changed jobs and became a teacher later.) Meryl saw that my need was to be saved, but she did not go at me to change my ways. She asked two other girl friends, who were also born again, to pray for me to be saved and taken out of Satan's clutches. Mother said, "Why don't you make friends with Meryl? She's a nice girl." I said, "No! She's cold, aloof, and stand-offish, not my sort of friend at all." (Now I know that the demons in me recognised the Christ in her and that they wanted to keep us apart because God had chosen her to be his servant to lead me to Jesus. Can darkness have fellowship with Light?)

After a while Meryl asked me to go with her to *The Hayes Conference Centre* in Swanwick, Derbyshire where a group from *Lee Abbey Community* were leading a course from Friday night to Sunday afternoon. I thought it might get me out of my rut and I might make friends with someone, so I went with her. I had never met such a lovely, loving, kind, helpful lot of people! Time went by too quickly.

Meryl then suggested I would like to go to *Lee Abbey* for an Easter week's holiday, where she had been for a holiday herself, so she knew what it was like. I thought I might meet a boy who could be a husband, for this was the desire and longing of my heart. The only thing I felt I could do for the rest of my life was to be a housewife and mother, and I needed someone to look after me when my parents died. They were by then in their seventies so might not live much longer. Father said I could have his Morris Minor car to go down to *Lee Abbey* with Meryl. We booked some weeks ahead because it gets very booked up as it is so popular.

At *Lee Abbey* Meryl and I shared a bedroom with two other ladies for the ten days holiday house party at the end of March and beginning of April. Easter was early that year. The spring time, the sea views, the walks and the food were all excellent. There were morning and evening gatherings for talks and for singing hymns, but you could come or go as you pleased. There was no compulsion. The leaders of the week were a Mr. Leslie Sutton and his wife Phyllis. Mr. Sutton gave a talk on deviation religions – those that did not accord with Bible truth. Among them was Spiritualism. I wanted to say to him that he had got it all wrong and to tell him of my own experiences to prove it, but I dared not speak out in front of all those people in the lounge. I went to him afterwards and asked if I could speak to him some time after lunch. He said, "You have a car, don't you?" I replied, "Yes". "Then we can go a run round the country lanes and have a chat then." I started out with Meryl, Leslie and Phyllis in the car. Leslie said, "Jo, when you see the first lay-by pull into it and we will have a prayer together. I found one and pulled in and stopped the engine. Leslie said, "Jo, God has got a much better life for you than the one you are living now. We will pray that, before the week is out, you will find what that life is. Now drive on." They would meanwhile pray for me, and the Community would pray for me. (There is more power through agreement against the enemy when two people pray, while believing the same thing, than when one person prays alone.)

On the last night Meryl asked me if I would become a Lee Abbey Friend. "What does that mean?" I asked. "You give your life to Jesus, just like the disciples did, and serve him for the rest of your life." I said, "No! I read the Bible, say my prayers, sing in the choir and am secretary of the British and Foreign Bible Society. God would not want more from me than that." She did not try to persuade me and we went to lunch. Afterwards I had a hymn on my brain. It would not go away. The words kept repeating over and over again. The hymn was, "O worship the Lord in the beauty of holiness, bow down before him his glory proclaim." [1] The "bow down, bow down, bow down" was loud and clear. I said to Meryl, "I have this on my mind and it won't go away. What do you think it means?" She said, "That's God telling you to go to the Friends' service and bow down at the altar rail and in your own words say you will give your life to him." I said, "Well, if it's God speaking to me, I had better obey and go." (Parents like mine who bring up their children to obey them make it easier for them to obey God and those in authority in later life.)

The 5.15 p.m. service came, and people went for the laying on of hands to the altar. I said, "Well, Lord, I've had ten years of hell and misery. If serving you can be any better, you can have my life and do what you like with it, but you must guide me every step of the

---

[1] John Samuel Bewley Monsell (1811-1875)

way." There was no vision or sudden light or feeling different. That was all to come a little later.

I had agreed to meet Leslie and Phyllis after supper to tell them about my occult life. But, when I started to tell them, all I got out was that in 1957 a boy friend was killed in a car accident. No more was said because I started to cry and was not in control of it, so I said, "I'm sorry, I can't go on. I'll go to my room." Meryl came with me and, while we were on the stairs, we passed a Community member coming down. She said, "Oh, Jo, what's the matter?" I did not reply, but Meryl said "Come and pray with her and me." So I was on the bed crying and saying "Don't stop it, it's got to come out." What "it" was I didn't know, or the name of it, but, when the crying ceased, "it" had obviously gone. I felt as if a very heavy load had been lifted off me. I felt happy, not depressed, and went straight to bed and fell fast asleep.

Instead of continuing to cry, or taking ages to get to sleep or having dreams, nightmares, or astral travelling I slept soundly. I woke early, at 5.00 a.m. singing another hymn, "I bind unto myself today the strong name of the Trinity".[2] I wanted to go out and dance by the sea, but considered the others in the room, so started to read my Bible instead. The Holy Spirit lit up the truth in a way I had not experienced before. I went to breakfast and saw Leslie and Phyllis to say "Goodbye" as it was going home time. They said, "We are so glad to know you have found the start of God's plan for your future life. Meet up with Meryl, do Bible reading and study and pray together. Take a notebook and write down everything God shows you – answers to prayer, anything to thank God for, and you will have something to look at should you come on hard times spiritually."

We said farewell and returned home. Our house, *"The Park"*, overlooked the entire long driveway, out to the nearest road. Mother was watching for us and saw our car turn into the drive. She came outside to greet us. Her first words were, "What happened? You look twenty years younger!" I said, "I have given my life to Christ. I don't yet know what that involves but I do know I shall never be the

---

[2] Ascribed to St. Patrick, tr. C. F. Alexander

same as when I left here." Oh the joy after the sorrows! I sang songs of worship while washing up and doing chores. It was the 4<sup>th</sup> April 1964.

## Lee Abbey Reunion and a Return Visit

There was a *Lee Abbey Reunion* the following October at St. Paul's Church in London. I went to this and had a very interesting experience. Someone I had met at *Lee Abbey* invited me and several others along to her flat for a meal. The friend she lived with had also invited friends. They had not prepared food for so many. We said grace over the food and it went round everyone with some left over. We knew it was a miracle like the feeding by Jesus of the 5,000.

In June another year, I returned to *Lee Abbey* for a holiday, calling on the way to see a friend I had made on Pilgrimage to the Holy Land in May 1996. Frances showed me her photographs, and asked me for copies of my slides as she only had prints. She was being asked to go to give talks in her area and slides would be so much more interesting. (I don't know where the slides went to after Frances's death. They may still be in use as mine are today.)

There was a job of work for me at *Lee Abbey* which unfolded as the week went on. Someone who was sharing my bedroom was there to sort out a problem in her life. She was tossing and turning and obviously troubled about something, so I got out of bed and went over and asked if I could be of any help, but, apart from prayer and laying on of hands, there was little I could do. I did not want to pry into her affairs, and the middle of the night was not the best time to talk anyway.

The next day there was a *Lee Abbey* Friends' service, like the one held there before my conversion and previously described. Afterwards some people, including my room-mate and a friend who had come with her, stayed behind talking. There were four persons, plus myself, in the chapel. I felt moved to offer them all the laying on of hands as they were up at the altar in a long row. I put both hands on the first person, then my left hand on the lady and my right hand on the man, then both hands on the last head. I do not know why I did it that way but it just seemed right. I learnt afterwards that they took that as God's signal that they were to get married, which they did. After their honeymoon they came to tea at *The Heritage* where I then lived, and thanked me for deciding the matter for them. We don't know how God may use us privately or publicly for folk to make such momentous decisions. What if I had not followed the Spirit's leading to lay hands on them in the Chapel and at the Altar, too? I had not had permission from the Community. What if I had been fearful of doing it?

While on another visit to Lee Abbey when I was a married woman, the couple who had the room next to ours heard that we were from Astwood Bank. They asked if we knew a nurse called Jean Bendall who worked at Evesham hospital. When we told them we did not know her they said what a nice Christian girl she was and gave us her address. She was to become a friend of ours and God used her to help us when I was expecting my daughter.

**A New Home – "The Heritage", Broome**

When my grandfather died he left me and my sister, Diana, a farmhouse and adjoining cottage, with a fold yard and some farm buildings. The buildings had been let in the recent past to *Midland Accredited Stations Hatcheries Ltd.*, who incubated eggs, hatched chicks and sold them at a few days old. The company went into liquidation, and when we inherited the buildings they were all in a dilapidated state. We sold the farmhouse and the cottage and used the money to convert the C19$^{th}$ wagon house with granary loft, along with the C20$^{th}$ annexe that was previously the chicken sexing room, into a bungalow.

We had to get planning permission to do this. The Parish Council supported our application but the County Council opposed it on the grounds that it would open the way to many more such applications to convert agricultural properties into dwelling houses. Our solicitor cited precedents where permission had already been granted. The County Council also stated that it was a traffic hazard and stationed an employee to record the traffic of a combine harvester and trailer to a nearby field. We argued there was more traffic when the buildings were used for the Hatchery business than for residential purposes. They also said a dwelling would increase the population, but as we had sold the farmhouse and cottage as a single unit, instead of two houses, we argued that the number of households would be unchanged. Villagers were asked, at a hearing in the Church Hall, if they had any objections. The Government Inspector who heard the case visited the site and approved our application.

14

I knew it was God's will for me to leave my parents and live with my sister, as the same words were given that moved Abraham from Ur to tell me to move too. We had a local builder and it was fun to fit rooms into the empty shell. I had a single bedroom, bathroom, lounge-dining room and spare bedroom. My sister had 2 bedrooms, a lounge-dining room and a shower room. We shared a kitchen and the hall. There were doors to the exterior at the front and the back of the bungalow.

My father erected a prefabricated concrete garage for my 1100 Austin car, and Diana had a garage in part of the old barn that formerly housed farm implements.

We tried to keep the exterior appearance as it had been for years, retaining the wagon house iron pillar and beam in the end that faced the village. We retained the iron window frames but replaced these later when we installed double glazing. God had already provided the cash for the alterations and for furniture and household things. Linen and crockery were provided for a very reasonable sum from my mother's cousin who had to give up her flat to live out her old age in a hotel room. She said, "Take what you want and donate what you can." My mother's sister died and left us £150 which paid for flooring tiles and carpet. Diana was already provided for, having sold a bungalow where she had previously lived.

Christmas Eve 1966 was one I shall never forget, as my sister and I moved into *The Heritage* to sleep there after the midnight Communion service in Broome Church. The joy and excitement of being in my own shared home on such a night was one of God's special blessings. (God had not then told me then that I would be moving two years later to get married.) While at *The Heritage* I could have ministers to stay and could hold meetings in the large lounge. It was also a stepping stone for me to learn to live away from my parents and for my parents to get used to my sleeping and living away from them. However, I went every morning to help them with cleaning, cooking, gardening or shopping. I was free for the rest of the day. My sister and I both desired to have the house blessed, and the minister came on 5th January 1967 to do this for us. God opened the doors for me, so I could witness, or talk to groups, to people in their homes, or to church fellowships. What a wonderful God and how he moves in "a mysterious way his wonders to perform"!

## CHAPTER TWO: HEALING MINISTRY
### The Guild of Health

Before I was born again, my Aunt Norah in Scotland had sent me a Brother *Mandus' Crusader Magazine*. How she got hold of it I don't remember, but the hand of God was on it. On the back page was a list of Guilds that held healing meetings or services. It gave the Guild of Health in Birmingham that held its meetings in the Friends Meeting House in the Bull Ring in Birmingham. The secretary, Mrs. Cameron, lived in the next village to Broome. "Lucky", I thought. I wrote to her saying I was very interested in healing and could I go with her to one of their meetings. She replied, "Yes" and she would pick me up for the next one which was in February 1964. I enjoyed that very much and asked if I could join and go regularly. Little did I know that it was going to be thanks to Mrs. Cameron that I would meet the man God had for me as a husband at her home. Nor did I know that I would be their May speaker and become their secretary for tape recording.

A few days after my return from *Lee Abbey*, I went to hear George Bennett at St. Philip's Cathedral in Birmingham. I also went to more meetings at the Guild of Health.

When the Guild learnt of my conversion and vision they asked me to be their speaker. Their talks were usually very profound and on the healing ministry only, so I wondered how mine would go down. My friend, Meryl, came with me and confirmed that all that I said was true. It was gladly accepted and I made friends there who were friends for many years until they died. My talk was taped, on the old reel-to-reel tape, not the cassette variety. I think it is still along with others in their cupboard.

The Guild asked me to become their tape recording secretary and to do any copies if required. I did not possess a recorder myself so prayed about how to get one. God had one already waiting for me in the hands of Dr. Pearce, my father's eye specialist, who came to my parents' farm sometimes with his friend. I mentioned I wanted a recorder in his presence and he said, "I want to sell mine, a Grundig, to get a more modern one." He said I could buy the Grundig off him for £17.00, which I did. Recording on tapes led to my taking tapes to people's homes for them to hear good talks. Many were aged, infirm and housebound so they could not go to meetings. Some were sick, so I took tapes about the same illness that they had to encourage them to believe so their own needs could be met and prayers answered. A lot of friends were made this way. I found that God gave me just the amount of work that I could comfortably undertake. As I look back I see that it was his grace that was sufficient for each day. One of the words I received from the Lord was to look after widows. There were plenty in the close in Redditch where I lived after my marriage. Retirement bungalows were built near our house. I was very involved with two ladies. I did errands and shopping for them, collected prescriptions from doctors, took them to hospital or the dentist and cleared their drives and paths when it snowed.

Two of us attended a Guild meeting in Birmingham when the dreadful bombing by "The Birmingham Six" took place. While I was at the *"Queensway"* round-about, the Lord said, "You are entering danger city". We were forewarned but did not know how to avoid the danger, so asked for his covering and protection. While the speaker was talking about the Abortion Bill, there was the most almighty thud followed by sirens. The chairman decided to close the meeting as it was obvious something very serious had taken place. We started home in the car, only to be diverted by police. We saw a number of ambulances going by. We had to take the Stratford road, instead of the Redditch road out of Birmingham, and only after we got home did we hear the news of the bombing. Others, who heard the news earlier, were much relieved at our return.

**Redditch Guild of Health**

When a Church Army worker came to Redditch we became friends. He was also interested in healing so he helped us to start a branch of the Guild of Health in Redditch. It went very slowly at first. It met a need for a few regulars, but not many came. After prayer we decided to close it down.

**Witnessing and Healing**

Since I wanted to learn more about healing I went to *Thorpe Hall,*[3] Northamptonshire, Mildred Blower's home of healing. She had been healed of a back problem in a miraculous way. She wrote a book about it and started healing work herself. The book was called

---

[3] Breakthrough: the Story of Jane, Arthur James Ltd., 1962

*"Breakthrough"*. I learnt a lot. One thing we were told to do was to put two shillings and six pence in a box every time we talked about our problems or illnesses. It stopped so many moans and groans!

On my return from the *Thorpe Hall* conference, I went to a gathering of the *Bible Institute* at Birmingham Central Hall. It was my first experience of so many believing Christians all praising God.

In the year 1964 I was asked by various churches to give my testimony. (I got known by word of mouth.) Bromsgrove Methodist Church was one and Henley-in-Arden another. Afterwards I was asked to pray for healing and to visit to sick and house-bound people. I was still involved with the Women's Institute as a speaker and judge at their shows. I talked about Christmas decorations. However, these talks also often led to my witnessing to individuals about what Jesus had done in my life.

At a Guild of Health Conference *High Leigh* I was full of joy, learning more about ministry to others and how others served the Lord in healing ministry. One minister was a lovely man of God, the Reverend Robert Neil, who had written a book, *Healed in the Name of the Lord*, which I obtained from him. He came from Worksop in Nottinghamshire. We became friends and he was a great help to me, being my spiritual adviser and guide. God led us to meet later on at his rectory, but other things happened before this took place.

My sister, Diana, at a time before we acquired *The Heritage,* shared her home in High Wycombe with a nurse. This nurse met me and asked me to visit several of her patients who were ill with cancer, as I had a healing gift and tapes. I was willing to do what I could. I had nothing to give of myself but love. The first patient was very near death and all I did was love her, love God and put the two together. I then played a fifteen minute tape of Brother Mandus to her. Not a word was spoken between the lady and me. I left after half an hour and went home, but a week later I had a letter from the woman's daughter asking me to go back to see her. Her mother had died in complete peace.

She wanted to know what I said and did. So I returned a week later and also called upon a second patient. God had given me guidance that it was his will for me to go and see them. In fact God was behind everything I did, the journey, the ministry and the Gospel sharing. I had dropped my Bible on the floor when rushing to leave, and the book marker fell out. I just shoved the marker in anywhere and left.  The nurse had just come to give the second patient morphine injections when I arrived, so I had to wait in the lounge. The wife came in with a cup of tea and I told her that God had told me, that he would be healed in three days. I did not know if it would be by a miracle and he would live, or whether he would be healed by death.  The nurse said, "You may go up to him now."  I went upstairs to his room.  He had cancer behind the eye so his eye was pushed out of its socket.  I had not been prepared for this and hope I did not show any reaction to him.  I said, "May I pray for you?" He said, "No."  I said, "Do you mind if I sit in the chair and read my Bible?"  He said, "No."  I thought I would read where I had shoved in the book marker after I dropped the book.  I was reading Romans, chapter eight, when suddenly he said "You may read me that much" and held up his thumb and first finger separated by about three inches. So I read on from where I had got to, verse 25, to the end of chapter 8.  The verse he needed to hear was verse 26, "The Spirit helps us in our weakness. We do not know what we ought to pray for, but the Spirit himself intercedes for us with groans that words cannot express."  He said, "You can pray for me now."  I did, and left and came home.  A few days later his wife wrote to say it was just as I had said it would be. Three days after my visit he had received peace and died.

**Enid Wright a local asthma sufferer**
January 1965 saw the funeral of Sir Winston Churchill and I offered to go round the village of Broome to collect for his memorial fund. This led me to a home where the owner shouted, "Do come in! I can't come out to you."  I went in and the lady, Mrs. Enid Wright, said she suffered so badly from hay fever and asthma that she could not go out when pollen might be in the air.  She was virtually house-bound.  She had not had a holiday for four years.  I explained to her that Jesus was still healing people today and that I had got a tape, recorded at the Guild of Health meetings, of a lady whom he had healed of asthma.  If she would like to hear it I would take it and the recorder to her home.  She replied, "Oh, yes, please" and asked if she could invite a few friends and relations to hear it at the same time. A date was fixed and all attending said how interested they were and could they hear about some more healings.  I said, "By all means,"

and so a village tape ministry was started at her house. This was in April 1965.

One day when I was at Enid's house she told me she often woke with an asthma attack in the night. I said, "When that happens, start to pray for someone else. Then you won't become so fearful of it getting worse." That night I went to bed and prayed for her as she was on my prayer list. At 2.00 a.m. God woke me and said, "Mrs Wright's praying for you now." I went to her next morning to thank her for doing so. She was amazed to hear God had woken me and told me. She was a great prayer warrior for me after that until she died. She was also able to come to our wedding. Even though the church was full of flowers she had no hay (or pollen) fever. Healing for that had taken place already. She had first-hand knowledge that prayer was effective and answered. She even went on holiday to Scotland to visit relations after being house-bound for four years and this was a great joy to her.

**Healing at Hildenborough Hall**

*Hildenborough Hall*, Sevenoaks, Kent, is a place where I met people who became friends, and who are all still friends today. I also met and felt drawn towards a boy who held very similar beliefs and was also involved with healing. He came out to see me at *The Park* where I was then living with my parents. However, after an interval of time and prayer we knew we were not the ones for each other in God's scheme of things. He had to come for business at Worcester, so did not stay for the night with us. There were things happening, phone messages did not get through, transport broke down, letters arrived late, which indicated to us that we should break off the relationship before it got more serious. How important it is to let God say yea or nay in affairs of the heart! It saves much heartache and wasted time.

There was an Easter House Party I attended at *Hildenborough Hall*. There was wonderful teaching and I learned so much about working for the Lord, fellowship with other believers, giving witness, and helping to meet other people's needs. One need was that of the girl with whom I shared a bedroom. She was in a bunk bed above me. She saw me writing up my diary and my thanks for answers to prayer every night. She became envious of how much I had to write about. I sensed an atmosphere between us. I guessed it was the 'Old D' trying to pull us apart when God had put us together for his

21

purposes to be worked out. I realised she needed healing for her resentment and offered her the laying on of hands which she refused. That did not stop me from laying my hands underneath her bed and praying for her silently. Suddenly, at 2.00 a.m., she asked for help. Confession was made, the laying on of hands was given and healing resulted. Praise the Lord! There was another person who, hearing of this healing and my visions and dreams and dramatic conversion, was struggling because he had not had any such experiences and had started to doubt his own conversion. I was given a word for him, not to struggle and strive for the same things or experiences others had, but to trust God to give him what was best for his own life and walk with God.

**Healing on a Train**

The end of the week at *Hildenborough Hall* came all too quickly and, having said goodbyes, I set off for the station. I offered myself to the Lord for any work he had for me to do that day. I looked around at the crowds gathering for the train to see if there were any people in need of a word from the Lord, perhaps the lame, blind, or wheelchair users. There were none of those. Having asked the Lord to place me in the seat of his choosing in the carriage, I got on and took the first seat by the window. The train was so full there were people standing along the corridors as well as filling the available seats. I do not smoke so was in a non-smoking compartment. Conversation was slow to start with, but gradually people opened up to each other. Opposite me was a coloured lady with her daughter. She disclosed that she had been to London to see a Harley Street specialist for her daughter who suffered severely from hay fever and asthma. The child, whom I guessed to be about 11 years old, needed help as she could not go out to play; she was so allergic to grass lawns. I sent up arrow prayers to God, asking if this was the job of work he wanted me to do. If so, would he please empty the compartment of people so I could talk to and pray with this lady and with her daughter? If there were other believers he could leave them for "agreement powers" but they must approve the ministry of the laying on of hands. As the journey progressed to Birmingham others gradually got off at intermediate stations. Two new people got in. I suggested that as the child was in need of help, if those present did not object, I would pray and lay hands on her. All agreed, so the ministry was given. I said to the mother, "I will give you my address and if the child is not healed you can contact me again." I never heard another word, so I presume she was healed and there was no need for her to keep in touch. I gave God thanks for the healing on the train near Birmingham station.

## Mrs Carter

I was vacuuming my mother's lounge carpet when I was used to help another lady. I heard in a strong, clear, voice, "Go to Mrs. Carter now!" I told Mother I had to go to see someone and would be back to finish the carpet later. I got to Mrs. Carter's and she answered the door. I said, "What's the matter? I've had a call from God to come and see you now." She said, "Come in and look. I was about to commit suicide through an overdose of tablets with a cup of tea to swill them down." She realised that God's love stopped her doing it and she joined the tape group I mentioned earlier and became a different woman in a short space of time.

## Mrs Ward

For their summer meeting the Women's Institute entertained handicapped people. We took them round the village in their wheel chairs to see beautiful gardens and the very pretty church and to have tea in the old school before they were taken back home. I befriended a lady, Mrs Ward, whom I had taken round the village. She came from Quinton and God said I was to visit her at her home. She kept her door shut and locked unless she knew someone was coming and the day and the time. One day I felt I should go urgently to see her, so I wrote a postcard saying I would be calling on her at 3.00 p.m. the next day. In those days you could rely on post reaching its destination the next morning. When I got to her she said, "Oh, Miss Pheysey, I've been praying for you to come. My light bulb has gone and I can't get up to put a new bulb in. I'm afraid of the dark and no one else would have come to see me. It's not their day." So God saved her from the dark by telling me to go before darkness fell. Who says we have not got a loving, caring, heavenly Father who knows every need and will answer before we call!

Mrs Ward was afraid to go outside her home. She had once, when in a shop, had her crutch knocked from under her by a young lad with long, pointed, shoes. She fell and broke her hip. She did not want to risk that happening again, so I took Pastor North, one of the godly pastors I knew, to see her. Pastor North told her the following story in which she could see herself as "the lady". "A guide had taken a bus load of people to see the Niagara Falls. The party all put on waterproofs as they were to be taken behind the falls where the spray would wet them. There was a rope ladder by which to cross from one side to the other. They all started across, but one lady was so terrified that she stopped and clung onto the ropes when she was half way over. The guide was counting heads on the far side and when he found he was one short he went to look for her. There she was, unable to move for fear! The guide said, 'Lady, give me your hands and I will take you across.' She gave one hand but still clung to the rope with the other. He said, 'I can only lead you over when you give me both your hands. Then there will be nothing to hold you back.' She gave him both hands and they crossed over the water safely."

Mrs. Ward said, "I can see myself as that lady." Pastor North replied, "If you give Jesus everything, holding nothing back, He will guide you through the rest of your life, through all your troubles and difficulties." She immediately saw the point and gave her heart to the Lord. She lost her fears and I was then able to drive her out and about in the countryside.

The needs of Mrs Carter and Mrs Ward taught me to answer when God calls, as it can be a matter of life or death. Years later God told a doctor to return from his holiday a day early because someone would need his help and it was a matter of life or death. He obeyed. That person was me. All the cases showed God watching us. His eye is on the sparrow and I know he watches you.

**Healing at Swanwick**

I visited *The Hayes*, Swanwick, in Derbyshire, in November 1965 for a weekend conference where God used me in a wonderful way to meet people. I had gone up to my room for a rest in the free time in the afternoon. I told the Lord I would divide the free time into three parts. I would walk in the lovely grounds, I would be quiet and pray, and I would read a book on my bed. I had done the first two and was about to read the book when instructions were given to go back down among the people. There was a job God wanted me to do. I took my book with me and went to the lounge and sat where there

24

was an empty seat beside me. I thought God could then bring the person he had in mind to sit by me. My book was on healing. A lady came and sat beside me and, when she saw the title of the book, she asked if I knew anything about healing. I told her what I knew and she informed me that she was an epileptic and wanted the laying on of hands for this. I said that I knew the organiser of the conference and that I would try to see him to ask if this request could be met. On going to bed that night, by a God-incidence, I bumped into the Revd. Robert Neil, a clergyman I knew. I asked if it would be possible to fit in a service of laying on of hands for healing, as there were people in the conference who wanted this. He was not there in an official capacity, but he said he would see what he could do. He had no authority to do this himself, but we would take it to the Lord in prayer before going to sleep that night. He would let me know what guidance he had and if it could be arranged. Since it was God's will, doors were opened and the service arranged. It was a beautiful service and many went forward for the laying on of hands. It was obviously meeting a lot of needs and I returned home thanking God for the experience.

**Introducing Babs Honey to the ministry of healing**

Having been a past chairman of the Women's Institute County Produce Guild I was invited as a guest at their yearly rally. I was pleased to accept, thinking I would meet old committee members over the lunch provided for us, enjoy seeing the show and listening to the speaker, Mrs. Honey who used to write articles for *The Farmers' Weekly*. When the time came I went along but had no idea of what God had in mind for me to do. There was another God-incidence.

In her talk Mrs. Honey mentioned she had a son who had been in a very serious car accident and was left badly injured. I happened to sit next to her over lunch and enquired if she had any experience of Divine Healing through the Laying on of Hands and of prayer asking for help from Jesus to heal the sick. "What's that?" she asked. I then told her of my involvement with the work and that if she was interested I could get someone I knew to visit her as she lived near Bath. I was thinking the Guild of Health might know someone in her area, and meanwhile I could ask for prayer for her son at their meeting and apply to headquarters in London for prayer there. I could send her some of the booklets they had printed on healing matters. Through this we corresponded and became friends, and later, after I was married and when I was expecting our child, my husband and I went to stay with her. She arranged for me to speak at a village hall on the subject of divine healing and then to return with her friends and family for more talk and questions at her home. This time was so used by God that we went on ministering into the very early hours, talking and leading people to Jesus.

God continued to open doors for me to give talks, meet the sick and housebound and continue learning more and more for myself.

**Four more families where healing was needed**

One family known to me had a twelve year old son, John, who was ill with cancer. I went often to see them as they lived nearby. They came with me to *Swanwick* after their son had died. This boy was posthumously awarded the Scout's VC for courage and endurance under great suffering. (The man I later married had been given the same award for his courage as a child, suffering under a long illness.)

The result of my giving another talk was to visit a little boy, only five years old, who suffered badly from epilepsy. We met weekly, either at his home or mine for eighteen months until he died (from a fit in the night).

Seeing and sharing so much suffering became a great burden for me, so I had to learn to go to the Lord and cast it all upon him and let him carry it. It was not for me to find solutions and answers to other people's problems, only to be his instrument and mediator and to be faithful to my calling, to obey his guidance and to be his witness before all manner of men.

It was when I was in Bridgenorth, listening to a speaker about healing, that the minister of the church heard me ask questions after the talk. He came across to me afterwards and asked if I would be willing to visit some of his parishioners who were housebound and sick. He then introduced me to a lady called Lily who was a friend of another lady, named Lucy, who was sick and housebound. Lily told me where her friend lived. We arranged a date for me to go there and play a tape of someone healed from arthritis, for that was her problem. Lily's husband would be able to drive her out from Bridgenorth to Lucy's home. This started regular meetings with tapes of different speakers and testimonies. Others joined us and this went on monthly until Lucy was so crippled she had to go to hospital to be treated. After years she was transferred to a hospital for treatment at the Droitwich brine baths.

**Rubery Church healings**

At the start of 1966 I was invited to speak at Rubery Church on a weekly basis, to give talks of 20 minutes, to pray for the sick and to hear reports on those who had had absent healing or healing by proxy. I had a book which listed names under headings of the place where I had met the people prayed for and I noted their physical or spiritual needs. This list was growing longer with every talk I gave. When the list got too long I placed the book between my hands and prayed for all to be in God's hands. He knew the needs and had the answers so I left it to him to do as he knew best. I later learned to ask the Holy Spirit to highlight ones for whom he wanted special prayer.

**Mothers Union Healing**

When I went to a Mothers Union meeting to speak on Divine Healing, a lady came up to me and asked if I could help her. I had mentioned in my talk that resentment, bitterness and hatred and an unforgiving heart could all be blockages to healing. She said she had all of them in her heart towards the man who had run into her son's motor bike, and to the man who was following and saw the accident but refused to give evidence against his friend. I gathered her son had been killed. Her trouble was that when she went past the garden shed in which her son's bike was kept she felt faint and ill.

I said, "If you can forgive and get rid of all these feelings in your heart towards these men then your symptoms will cease." I told her I would put her on my prayer list and ask God to give her a new outlook on the whole sad story and that he would fill her with his love and forgiveness towards them.

Some months later I asked God if I should continue to hold her up in prayer as no update news had been given to me by her or by anyone else. The Lord answered this prayer by directing me to take a different route to visit one of my sick ladies. As I drove along I saw someone going in the same direction carrying some heavy bags. I stopped to offer her a lift. When she got in she said, "Aren't you the lady who gave the Divine Healing talk to the Mothers' Union?" "Yes", I replied. She said, "You were quite right. I had a change of heart and got rid of my bad feelings. My fainting turns have ceased. I have been meaning to let you know." I told her how the previous night I had asked God if I should continue to pray for her. Now I knew the answer directly from her. It was God's perfect timing for us to meet on that road and for me to be influenced to stop and help her. Today you would think twice before offering lifts. This also shows God hears and answers prayers in unexpected ways. He could have reminded her to write or phone me but that would not have had the same impact on us both.

**Healing for a mourner**

A lady who had heard my testimony at the Guild of Health told her church fellowship to invite me to talk on healing at their meeting at Solihull. I was invited to lunch at the president's house beforehand so we could discuss and pray together over the afternoon's meeting.

When I offered the laying on of hands after the talk several people came forward. Some said what they wanted to be prayed for but others did not. While I was holding my hands on the head of one such lady I received words from a hymn, "Let not sorrow dim your eye, soon shall every tear be dry." When we were drinking tea afterwards I went over to her and said, "Do you mind telling me what you came up for when I laid hands on you, for I was given the words, 'Let not sorrow dim your eye'. Are your eyes growing dim?" She replied that that was her problem. I asked if she was grieving over someone. She told me that her niece had recently committed suicide and that she was very upset about this. I said, "I think you will find that your sight returns to normal when you are over the grieving process."

A year later I went back to speak there again and she came up to me and said, "It was just as you said it would be. My eyes are fine again now." Our thoughts, feelings and emotions do have a bearing on our health.

**Healing for Asthma**

In March we were invited to talk and pray with a 12 year old boy, John Mills, who suffered from Asthma attacks and who had had eczema earlier as a small child. His asthma came on when he went swimming, from sudden cold water. We were able to lead him to give his life to Jesus who healed him. His mother kept in touch for some time, especially when she heard that our own daughter had the same trouble as her son. She knew exactly how I would be feeling, having gone through it herself. As for me, I found it very hard to have seen answers and healing for John but not for our daughter. But God is sovereign and does what is just and fair for the good of all. If I had been to John after our daughter's birth, instead of before she was born, I would have understood the mother's and father's side much better as you know from experience what suffering does, especially in children.

**Healing for childhood leukaemia**

I was at a Methodist Church where I gave a talk on divine healing. I offered prayer for the sick and a lady asked me to pray for her son. A little boy came forward. There was no mention of what the prayer was required for, so I asked him to sit on my lap. I told him that Jesus was living in me so he was sitting on the lap of Jesus. I knew that Jesus had asked for children to be brought to him, so my prayer was one of thanks that since Jesus knew what the problem was he was able to put it right. The boy ran off and told his friends he had sat on Jesus' lap and had been healed. I learnt later from a letter from his mother that the problem had been leukaemia. When the boy had gone for his next check up his blood count was perfectly normal and the specialist who saw him could not understand why. It was still normal some years later. Thank God!

**Burns and a scald**

One day, before I was married, I took a tape of a sermon to an old couple in the village. When I arrived they were watching *Midlands News* on the television. I said, "Don't switch it off. I can wait a little longer." So we watched it to the end. One of the items in the news was that 3 men were in hospital very badly burned from molten metal that overflowed in a Black Country steel mill. I thought I should pray for them, but God had a very important lesson to teach me. We heard the tape of the sermon and I went home.

The next day we had a gathering of people for prayer at my mother's. I was out in the kitchen, making the tea. I then filled a hot water thermos from the boiling kettle and I over-filled it, pouring boiling water all over my hand. I was amazed, as I was not scalded. I went into the group saying, "I've just poured the boiling kettle water all over my hand and I have not been burnt." We thanked God for protecting me. That night I was praying and asked why those men were badly burnt and I was not? God said, "Look at Psalm ninety-one." There was the answer; because I was born again I had the protection of the Almighty; "Rest in the shadow of the Almighty.....He will deliver you from the snare of the enemy, covering you with his wings.... Because you have made the Lord your habitation there shall no evil befall you, for he shall give his angels charge over you in all your ways.....Because you have set your love upon me [you have all these things]....You call upon me and I will answer and deliver and honour and show my salvation."[4] Later this revelation was confirmed and reinforced by a dream that I had that I was walking along a path and flames were coming at me from both sides of the pathway and I walked through them and was not burnt.

I had two more similar experiences to this. One night, in our caravan, I was trying to save our battery (which was low) by not using the lights as there was a nearby street light. By that light I was filling my hot water bottle. Because I could not see very well I over-filled it and the water flowed all over my left hand. I gave it straight to Jesus and asked Harold to pray as I put my hand under cold water. There was no sign of redness or blisters afterwards.

On another occasion I turned on the grill but the wind blew it out. I went to get matches from the cupboard but, by the time I relit the grill, gas had built up. When I put the match to it flames back-fired over my hand. I claimed the Lord's promise that I would have his protection, and apart from a slight burning sensation the soreness soon went the more I praised the Lord.

---

[4] Verses 1-4; 9-11; and 14-16

## CHAPTER THREE: AIDS TO SPIRITUAL GROWTH
### The Bible
I had for some time been praying about doing an in depth Bible study, possibly by correspondence course as there were no courses in the village or locally. I wanted to understand more of God's word than my daily readings provided. I had sent some money to a Mr. Brian Williams to help run a crusade in Birmingham. He, in thanks, sent me a lovely Bible with pictures of the Holy Land and all that Jesus said printed in red. I still use it today, nearly 40 years on. It is the King James Version which I prefer as I feel it is nearest to the truth of the scrolls. It also has a concordance and maps at the back. This gift came unexpectedly and was another sign God was wanting me to do more study.

### The Navigators
The next step was taken when I discovered a pink slip of paper in my letter box. Written on it was, "If you want to do a Bible study, contact the Quinton Christian Fellowship, or Navigators" whose address was given. I thought the whole village would have had a pink slip too. I asked around and found I was the only one in the parish who had received it. This was another sign of God's hand at work especially for me. I wrote to both addresses and invited the person who had delivered the slip to my door to come to see me to say how he had come from Quinton just to my home. He came and said his pals were out distributing tracts in the area. They cycled down Belbroughton Lane on their way home and saw the signpost, "Private Road" at our driveway's end. He thought, "Private be blowed! I'll go there and take them a tract. It belongs to the Lord". So he came to the house and afterwards turned for home not realising the village was farther on. That's why others did not get the tract too. You never know whom God will choose to meet your needs, or when he will use you to meet another's need. The Navigators came as a group to hold a weekend camp on the farm with my cousin's permission. They sent me their correspondence course. It had subjects like Discipleship, Witness, Living in the will of God, etc. You had to find the answers to questions from your Bible so you got to know the books of the Bible as well.

God was wonderfully working in and for and through the Committed Christian Group held at *The Heritage* where I lived for a time. We heard about speakers from other Christians and Guilds and we were nourished by going to the Birmingham Youth for Christ *Fact and Faith* Films, and Guild of Health conferences and retreats. (Before my conversion I had not known of any of these.) We had our daily Bible reading notes and discussed what we had learnt from them. Books and tapes and visiting ministers all helped to satisfy our longing to know more about Jesus and his Kingdom.

**A promise from Jesus**

There was a lady living in Droitwich who was also a *Lee Abbey* friend. She invited me to her home when she had a lady from Oxford giving a talk to her group. I went along and was deeply moved by the speaker, but she was not the person the Lord sent me there to meet. During the talk I looked across the room at a lady seated opposite me and an inner voice said, "She speaks in tongues". For some time I had been searching and reading all about the gifts of the Spirit and wondering how I might set about getting them for myself. At the close of the meeting I went to her and spoke to her about my interest and search and asked if she could help me. Could she come to have a chat? She said she did speak in tongues but she did not live locally and was returning to Oxford but she would certainly pray for me and ask God to give me his gift. About a fortnight later a letter from her arrived which she had received from Jesus in direct answer to her prayer. It was as follows:

> "Tell this my child that I love her dearly and that I know her great heart of love for me. Tell her this gift of healing is a very precious gift and that she has pleased me well in that she has dedicated this to my service. Tell her that my hand of blessing is on her life and that I shall use her more and more for my glory.
>
> Tell her to seek to know my will in all things and that she shall know me and my voice when I speak to her without any shadow of doubt. Tell her that it is my desire that she should always love me with all her heart, mind, soul and strength and if she continues to do this no good thing will I withhold from her.
>
> Tell her that my blessing is on all she is attempting to do in My Name and that she will go on from strength to strength. She is very precious to me indeed."

On reading this I wept tears of joy and thanks that I should actually have a letter from my Lord. To think he should place such value upon me and my life and service to Him and the promise of blessing which has so wonderfully been fulfilled over all the years since it was written (on 3<sup>rd</sup> May 1966). I took notice of the conditions to love him totally, seek his will and hear his voice and follow it. Bless his holy Name! As I write, 37 years later, I can say He's kept His promise but I have failed to do all of mine.

**Visions and paintings**

Prior to going to *Lee Abbey* I had agreed to have a week's holiday with my Aunt Norah at a guest house in the Lake District. I reached the Lake District earlier than we had arranged to meet, so I decided to go to Lake Windermere to take photographs. (One of my German friends had given me a camera and I had joined the Kidderminster Photographic Society of which I was a member for seven years. I took both prints and slides and even learnt how to develop black and white films at the studio dark room in Kidderminster.) I always carried my cameras with me. I drove round the lake and saw a footpath that went down to the lakeside. I parked the car in a safe place and walked down to investigate the possibilities of getting pictures good enough for any competition. We had learnt how to compose a picture and how to get points of interest and subject matter and lighting to bring out the mood and atmosphere of a place. Thinking of these points I saw the perfect picture except that the clouds and sunlight were not quite right on the bulrushes and the mountains behind. I sat down on the grass to wait for the sunlight to move further round. I was very happy and at peace and felt I could have been beside the Sea of Galilee (I had not been to the Holy Land as yet, but saw it later in 1966[5]). I was half dreaming as I sat by Windermere. Suddenly, in the dream, I saw the water had footprints and the feet and ankles of someone walking along beside me. I said out loud, "There is only one person who walks on water and that is Jesus". As I spoke his name I heard him say, "I charge you to be an evangelist, to preach the Gospel and to heal the sick and to take the good news to all manner of men. Lo, I am with you always, even to the end of the age." Then all went back to normal. The water drops that fell from the feet of Jesus were like sparkling diamonds. I was told later it was his Shekinah or glory. This happened on 8<sup>th</sup> May 1964, and it made me very happy and excited. I felt I was in my

---

[5] See Appendix

seventh heaven. I told my Aunt, who thought I was over the top. I told my family on my return, "I've seen Jesus". I was so in love with him I no longer wanted or desired human love and never gave marriage another thought until 1968.

Another occasion I remember was seeing a lovely painting in a friend's dining room. My friend explained to me that, within the picture, there was a second picture made by the Holy Spirit. Only those who have been born again can see the one the Spirit painted. This was something new to me, I had not heard of such a thing. Later, however, this phenomenon was to occur in a painting I did, after my visit to the Holy Land, of the Sea of Galilee at sunrise. I had a photograph of the Sea, so later, when on holiday at *Lee Abbey,* I had time to make a painting of the scene. I took it home but was not satisfied with how I had painted the sun's rays. I had painted them like a black and white "zebra" road crossing, all the same width and strength and length. When I saw a sunset I realised the rays should be varied in length, strength, and colour. So I got out my paints and repainted the sky over the Sea of Galilee and hung the revised painting in my lounge. One day my mother and a minister were having tea with me. While I was out of the room, making the tea in the kitchen, the minister asked Mother, "Who painted this picture?" She replied, "My daughter did." He then said, "There is great spiritual significance in it." After he had left my Mother told me what he had said. That night I asked God why, when I painted it, I had not seen what he saw hidden in the picture? God showed me straight away Christ "risen with healing in his wings", at the right hand of God, surrounded by angels and doves in the clouds. Only spirit filled people see what the Spirit painted in the sun's rays and the clouds.

I learnt later about a man who became the "painting preacher", painting while he preached. This artist had been a painter and decorator. While he was stripping paint off a door, he suddenly saw that he had been used to make a picture of Christ on the Cross. This led to his giving his life to Jesus. A cousin of mine was given one of this man's paintings and he told us about them. I was by then married, and my husband wanted to order one for me. We specified that it should contain mountains, a lake, and silver birch trees. That was all.  When we went to collect the one he had painted for us there were several paintings on display, but we knew immediately which was ours.  The colour of the lake matched the colour of our lounge carpet, and the birch trees had colours like our curtains.  When we hung it up, I saw my husband, and his dogs and me hidden in the snow on the mountain top.  There were three mountain peaks, three guide dogs, with Jesus and the two of us – all threes.  The birch trees in the picture were on an island in the lake.  My husband had rowed me round an island on a lake when we were on our honeymoon.

## Godly People
### The Suttons

The first people I invited to come and stay and to speak to the group I had started from friends and relations and villagers were Leslie and Phyllis Sutton who had ministered to me at *Lee Abbey*.  We had great blessing, but the enemy attacked to try to destroy it by spoiling the harmony and unity and by making people misunderstand each other in various ways.  It was a mixed group, both sexes, young and old, and it was an eye-opener to me to see how the spoiler works.

Leslie and Phyllis Sutton came to stay again in March to speak at the Guild of Health and at a coffee morning for ministers and a ladies afternoon meeting.  For over 6 months I had been suffering from a bodily complaint and was receiving treatment from doctors and specialist for what they thought to be an allergy to soap powders and to materials worn against my skin.  The treatment was to no avail.  When I mentioned this problem to Leslie and Phyllis they prayed over me with the laying on of hands.  They had in the Spirit that my trouble was caused by my praying for someone who was possessed and that I must stop praying for him.  He was a past boy friend who had asked me to marry him and I had declined.  Later, after I was born again, I met him at the doctors and he asked me to pray for him which I did, without thinking of it being wrong to do so.  When I ceased praying for him the problem left me straight away.  Doctors don't have all the answers especially if the problem has spiritual causes. I learnt a lesson through this that not all people should be on our prayer list.  There are some we are meant to pray for and some not, depending on our own spiritual knowledge, and development.  We should first seek God's guidance.

## Mike Hall

As I was sitting at a conference, talking to someone next to me, a man went by in front of us. The Lord said, "I want you to link up with that man." We were put into the same group for discussion and sharing and found we had much in common. Before we parted this man, Mike Hall, said, "I think God wants you to come and speak to my house group. You pray and I'll pray about it. There is no need to say 'yes' or 'no' because we will both have the same answer". I had the date and place to go to if the answer was "Yes". This was an entirely new way of working and trusting in God. I felt his answer was "Yes" and went over 100 miles to Mike's home in time for lunch. The meeting was to be held in the afternoon. I had no idea of what size or kind of group it would be; believers, unbelievers, or mixed. I thought, as they were gathering together, what a noisy lot they were. I gave them my testimony and there was dead silence when I finished. Somehow God had used me to get through their brainy heads and hard hearts. They were all men from a factory close by. I learnt later that one of them had sought after God from hearing what he had done in my life. The link was kept open for further visits and talks that God had in his plan for our lives. Mike was a school teacher when I knew him first and later he trained for the Ministry at Ridley Hall. He subsequently married and had children. There were further visits which will be described in a later chapter.

## Alec and Mary Learmont

In June of 1966 I met a wonderful couple of visiting evangelists, Alec and Mary Learmont from Florida. (Mary's nom de plume was Mary Light.) They took a healing service at St. Saviour's Church, Hagley. I went along to hear them and was very impressed with their ministry and with the message they gave. After the service I invited them over for a meal to get to know them better and to learn from them how they came to do healing services. This was in God's plan as he used them in future visits.

When Mary and Alec were in Australia on a healing ministry tour they met the Revd. Eric Barker. He was single and my age and they said I should invite him over to stay and they would write a letter of introduction. The couple thought Eric would make a suitable husband for me. He was coming to England with his mother anyway. I only had one spare room for guests at *the Heritage* but my parents offered to give Mrs. Barker bed and breakfast. It was agreed that the Learmonts should write to the Revd. Barker suggesting he came and talked to the Guild of Health and stayed with me and his mother could stay nearby with my parents. This invitation was accepted.

All was settled and they arrived. I had arranged for him to talk on the subject of Healing to a ministers' gathering. He was also to preach at Evensong at Broome. However we made some time for sight-seeing in Stratford, Worcester, and Coventry while also allowing him time to prepare his talks. On the way to a Guild of Health meeting we had a slight car accident on a dual carriage way. A foreign driver thought I would pass him on the left, but although I had sounded my horn to warn him I was overtaking, he still pulled out to take a right turn. I swerved to avoid him and landed up on the central reservation inches from a telegraph pole. We exchanged insurance details and he admitted he was in the wrong. Instead of continuing on our way I drove back home and asked if I could borrow my father's car in case mine was dangerous to drive. (Fortunately there was nothing more serious than a dent made by his bumper the whole length of the passenger side of my car.) All this made us late arriving at the meeting.

The Barkers' visit came to an end, but we did see Eric again after his mother had died and after I had married. He said he would never have married. It would have been too much to ask any girl to share the life he lived, constantly changing homes in the hot Australian outback.

On a later visit to Broome, Mary and Alec Learmont were invited by the Rev. David Copley to St. Kenelm's Church, not far away. After this they started a healing group there. People came to the communion rail and stayed in the sanctuary if they wanted the laying on of hands for healing. Those who did not want it returned to their seats after communicating. This was a good way to introduce the healing ministry to places that have no previous experience of it.

While Mary helped me in the kitchen to prepare meals she taught me to do everything as to the Lord, and to pray over and bless whatever I was doing. If ironing, pray for the person to whom the garments belonged, if washing up, give thanks for the food that had been eaten, for those who sold it, those who brought it, the growers who grew it and so on. She made some cookies and gave me the recipe so I could make them in future. She also said, "Don't burn the candle at both ends. Have a rest after lunch. It will pay off in the long run." She and Alec were both in their seventies by then.

Through Mary and Alec I was introduced to a Mr. and Mrs. Wood who lived at Kinver and ran a house group there. I took Mary and Alec to join the Woods on a journey to Aberystwyth for a healing conference. I stopped to have lunch with them in Kinver before they all continued on their way and I went home. It was through the Woods that I met the Rev. Grimshaw who was to introduce me to Pastor North who was a great help to me.

On another occasion, when I was married and living in Astwood Bank, Mary and Alec had come over to England again and wanted to stay with us and see the home that they had been instrumental in claiming for us. They had an itinerary already booked which allowed them to stop off and see us and then go on to *Green Pastures* in Bournemouth to do a healing work there.

We had arranged for a coach to stop at Astwood Bank to pick them up after their visit, but when the time came it did not stop in spite of our being at the road side with suitcases waving at the driver. I said I would drive them to Bournemouth as they had to be there that day. We phoned from home to see if *Green Pastures* could put us up as well as Mary and Alec and a dog. They said they had a room spare and would welcome the dog. The 200 mile drive made it a long, tiring, day but it was worth it for the sheer luxury of being waited on with breakfast in bed and no meals to cook or washing up to do. Then we benefited from all the spiritual food and fellowship. We were also able to visit an old pen friend of my mother. We returned refreshed, renewed and rested.

**Pastor North**

It was through the Rev. Grimshaw that I heard of Pastor George North. The Rev. Grimshaw told me to contact this pastor to get some more outside help to enable me to cope with the problems of so many sick, suffering, and needy persons. I was then only a learner myself, but was open to help and I invited him to come and stay with me. I knew he was a Pentecostal minister and was involved in a healing and deliverance ministry in the North. I suggested we meet at Stourbridge by the train and bus station, not thinking of the many roads and the amount of traffic there would be at that time even in those days. All I knew was that he would be driving a green Corsair car and would come from the North. I stood on a corner where I hoped to see all directions at once. As I turned my head to look under a bridge a green car came towards me and we both waved to each other knowing in the Spirit that we were the ones who were looking for each other. We were complete strangers, had never met, and did not know the other's age or appearance. In fact, Pastor North had a friend with him who was on the way to Exeter where he and Pastor North were involved in healing work.

That morning I took Pastor North to see my sick and house-bound folk, but in the afternoon the two friends drove on to Exeter. However, seeing my need of extra help, Pastor North promised to return three months later for four days to visit all of them and to give talks.

I learnt so much from watching this Godly, Spirit-filled, man minister to individuals according to their need, their understanding and their ability to follow his teaching. He spoke in parables like Jesus did, so the listeners could put themselves in the picture. For example, when talking about salvation he told one lady, "You and your husband have viewed this house, decided to purchase it, and when you had paid the price you got the keys, owned it, occupied it and used it. What if you had paid the price but the agent had not given you the keys? You were locked out? The house was yours but empty? When it was yours and you had got the key you filled it with beautiful things, gifts from the wedding, and it became a house that was beautiful to live in, a lovely habitation."

(Some readers will see the relevance of this story to Jesus who has paid the price for our sin and is standing outside waiting for us to let him in.)

Pastor North continued, "You must unlock the door of your heart and Jesus will come in and make you beautiful with his Spirit. He will make you a dwelling place for himself." When the lady heard it explained like this she said that she saw the truth in it and her need to admit Jesus, and in about 15 minutes she became a saved person.

Pastor North helped another lady whose need was to have her sins forgiven. He drew a picture for her to show that only Jesus can deal with sin. (I still have that picture.) Pastor North drew two trees with a cross between them. The one tree had crab apples whose fruit is bitter and sour. The other tree had nice, sweet, eating apples. He asked, "If you picked the fruit from one of the trees, would it change the tree?" "No, it would continue to bear the same kind of fruit next season according to its nature, either bitter or sweet." "What then can be done? The gardener will have to get an axe and chop the bitter tree down to the roots to cure the bitter fruit problem. He will then have to graft in a branch from the sweet fruit tree to change the nature of the bitter tree to sweet."

In our sinful state we are bitter and sour-natured. Only if Jesus comes with the Cross can sin be cut back so his Spirit can be grafted in to produce good fruit – love, joy, peace, gentleness, goodness, faithfulness, temperance and self-control. Our nature is then completely changed and we are new creatures in Christ Jesus.

Pastor North was a good listener. He heard what people said and also noticed what they did *not* say, which also spoke volumes. I took him to a friend's father who had been crippled by a stroke. This man could not see nor speak, only cry. How could one communicate under these conditions? Pastor North held his hand for the touch of Jesus and he then prayed in the Spirit who knows what to pray for when we don't. He then prayed naturally for peace. It was received and the man died soon afterwards.

This was another example of how we, as disciples, should treat everyone as an individual who is precious to God. By our manner, our speech and our touch, Christians are living letters to those who may only stand and observe. In those four days we went to Bridgenorth, Wolverhampton, Quinton, Harbourne, Hagley and Broome to take the love, comfort, hope and help of God to those in need. There was a change in everyone who met this wonderful pastor. Salvation, peace, confidence and healing are just some of the results that I came to know about after his visit.

**Margery Stevens**

Birmingham Guild of Health had a wonderful lady called Margery Stevens who had been healed of Multiple Sclerosis. She had had it so badly that she had to have everything done for her. She was strapped into a wheel chair so she did not fall out of it. She could

40

neither see, nor walk, and had cold hands and feet. Her mother washed her night and morning.

Many people, church members, relations and friends, had been praying for her. She had an assurance that prayer would be answered but she kept getting worse. Being a nurse she knew what was happening to her and what the end could turn out to be. However, she woke one morning knowing that she was healed, but, not wanting to give her mother a fright, she left things as normal. Her mother started to wash her and said, "Margery, your hands are warm!" She replied, "Mother, it's more wonderful than that. I'm healed!" Margery then got up, prepared breakfast, and then went and played the piano and, as she believed, she made a total recovery. She told me that Jesus saw the faith of all those who had prayed for her for some years, just as he had seen the faith of the friends of the paralysed man who let him down through the roof to be healed. The Bible tells us that Jesus had healed the man on the stretcher and he healed her. I still have a reel-to-reel tape recording of her talk given all those years ago but I do not know what happened to her later.

### The Rev. C. Tiquet and Dr. Ralph Ashmore

At a Guild meeting I made friends the speaker, the Rev. Tiquet. I had been told to pray for him while he was giving a talk, and afterwards I informed him of this. He replied that he suffered from duodenal ulcers and had been in great pain. He knew that I had been praying for him. He was a great help to me. He asked me to give testimony at a service at his church in Coleshill, Birmingham, and to join with him in the laying on of hands for healing in the service. This was the first time I had been asked to partake in ministry publicly in a church setting. God did a great work there. After he retired he went south, and I eventually lost touch with him.

In *1987* my husband was also a participant in a pilgrimage to the Holy Land. The leader was Dr. Ralph Ashmore who became a friend. He often stayed with us for two or three days at a time. Several times a year he would speak at house groups or fellowships. His entries in our visitors' book are a testimony in themselves, because I found out later that he was dyslexic and found it difficult to write and draw. I only discovered this when asking him to read a map for me when we were in a place I did not know. He died of cancer and we miss him very much.

41

**Other Aids to Spiritual Growth**

Ministers mentioned elsewhere in this book have also helped me, especially the Rev. Stan Woods and those who took me under their wing when I was a fledgling in ministry. I have also benefitted from Westminster Chapel School of Theology course, from the testimonies and books of others, from teachers, and from television and radio broadcasts and Bible study and prayer groups.

## CHAPTER FOUR: COURTSHIP AND MARRIAGE

In November 1967 I went to have tea with my parents. We sat in the dining-cum-sitting room with our tea on our laps watching the television programme, *"Blue Peter."* On the programme that day they showed the story of a blind man, Harold Bagby, whose guide dog, Kim, had taken herself and her master to the vet's surgery in Redditch. In so doing she had saved her own life as the enzymes in her liver had ceased working and she would have died in less than twenty minutes without proper treatment. The reason he was on TV was that the National Dog Owners' Association had awarded Kim their medal for this action. *Blue Peter* took up the story.

The picture showed Harold and the dog walking up the road from his home in Hunt End (a district in Redditch). Then they appeared live in the studio. When they mentioned Redditch I said to my mother, "Oh, he's local. Then I might meet him some day." This was a word of prophecy, though I did not know it at the time, and forgot all about it. I did meet him the following year, March 1968.

### First Meeting with Harold Bagby, 1968

At the start of the year 1968 I had no idea of how many more changes God would bring into my life; or how step by step he would guide me and provide for me to fulfil the plans he had already made for me. He was moving upon people, places and situations, upon relationships, money matters and other material things, so that all ran smoothly, and, as I obeyed, the next part followed on for me to walk in.

In the beginning of March, a lady I knew from the Guild of Health, named Mrs. Cameron, phoned me to ask if I would be willing to spare time for an evening meal and fellowship with others at her house on the 8th March. She wanted me to help a blind boy whose guide dog had bitten some official at a conference at Attingham Park. He had been asked to leave the dog behind for the next conference and go with a friend instead. However, the blind man did not want to do this. He had decided not to go at all, but to wait until this dog had died and then go with the next dog. He was feeling very depressed over it and Mrs. Cameron thought it would be a good idea to have a gathering on Friday night, the 8th March, the day he would have gone to Attingham, to help take his mind off it all. She asked if I could take some of my Guild of Health tapes to help cheer him up. I was not very keen to meet an Alsatian dog who had already bitten someone as I had been badly frightened when bitten through my clothes to the skin by an Alsatian in 1952 at the house of a friend's friend in Germany. However, I thought that perhaps the Lord wanted to use me to help restore his sight so I agreed to go.

The number eight, in Biblical terms, means new life, though I did not learn about Biblical numbers until later.[6] At the time of Mrs. Cameron's invitation I was not conscious of the date, the 8th, being special. (March, the third month of the year, however, has spiritual significance for me. March 4th was the date I was confirmed, and on March 9th, in 1989, I was restored from death to life.)

Mrs. Cameron had to go to fetch the blind boy and his dog, so she told me to wait in my car if she had not returned. The Lord timed our arrival at the same time. As we were walking into the hall the lid of my tape recorder fell to the floor. The boy, Harold Bagby, and I both bent down to pick it up and brushed against each other as we did so. (I learnt later that by that he knew that I had fuzzy hair and a pleated skirt.)

Mrs. Cameron had also invited her son, daughter-in-law and a friend, Mrs. Shearer, to share the meal and the evening with us. During the meal the talk ranged over a variety of subjects, but I myself, being me, mentioned the name of Jesus many times as I was accustomed to do, freely and naturally. To the others this was unheard of, and they thought I was "over the top". Afterwards, by agreement, we listened to Harold's tapes of *Jupiter* from Gustav Holst's "*The Planets*" instead of listening to my Guild of Health tapes. I thought, "Lord, why have you brought me here just to listen to this? When can I speak about you?" When the music had finished I suggested we should have a time of prayer and if anyone would like the Laying on of Hands I would be glad to oblige as this was a ministry with which God had entrusted me. Harold said he would like the Laying on of Hands. I stood behind him and placed both hands on his head. I had never felt tension like it before. I thought the pressures inside his head would explode. I had a word from the Lord, "In my light shall

---

[6] Number 4 can stand for the created order via the 4 compass points, 8 new life, linked to the last day of festivals or to special rituals, 3 the Holy Trinity or a period of 3 days culminating in a critical point (e.g. Matthew 12:40) and 7 can represent completion or perfection (e.g. Psalm 119:4).

ye see light." I thought this meant he would see again in the natural sense as well as in the Spirit. I asked him to pray for me and my work and service for the Lord which he readily and rapidly agreed to do. That concluded the meeting and we all went home.

As I drove back to my then home, *The Heritage,* I went over all I had heard about how Harold believed in the "isms" and "wasums", Satan's false religions from which I had been taken out and delivered. I had offered to take him home, but he was taken home by Mrs. Cameron's son, so there was no opportunity for me to speak to him further on his beliefs and faith but I took him to the Lord in prayer. I asked God, "How do I get Harold out of all this onto the right path and how do you want to restore his sight?" I felt that all would be all right if he gave his life to Christ and was born again. I told my mother I had met a blind boy who was in a lot of need and I did not know how to help him.

I had been asking what I should do next to get Harold onto the "straight and narrow path" that leads to heaven instead of "the broad way that leads to destruction". I was guided to invite him over to a Youth for Christ meeting at Birmingham Town Hall on Saturday 27<sup>th</sup> April and to stay the night after the meeting. I had said, "If this is your will, Lord, for me, he will ring up out of the blue." No sooner had I said that than the phone rang and it was Harold. He said, "Is that Joanna Vesey?" I replied that it was and that I had asked the Lord that if it was his will for me to invite him to stay a night, then he would ring me out of the blue.

Harold then told me the trouble he had had to get my phone number. He had rung Mrs. Cameron but she could not get access to her phone book because the floor in the room in which we had met had fallen in with dry rot and she had had to take out all her things while repairs were done. From memory she had said Jo Vesey had a Blakedown telephone number. Harold then asked his friend in the office to look me up in the directory but she could not find my name as it was Pheysey, not Vesey.

What happened next showed God was at work there. My number appeared all in Braille in front of him on the switchboard so he dialled it and I answered. So I did invite him to the Youth for Christ meeting and to my home afterwards for the night. My great uncle, who was at *the Heritage,* could be my chaperone, as my sister, Diana, who also lived there, was then in the United States of

America. Harold said his dog, Kim, was his chaperone. I said I would drive over to collect him at 2.30 p.m. on April 27th (just seven weeks after our first meeting) and take him home on the Sunday night. I suggested that on Sunday morning we should go to Longbridge Church where I was to speak to a ladies' meeting and later we should go for a walk on the Clent Hills.

**Second Meeting with Harold Bagby**

The day arrived and we went to the Youth for Christ meeting. Next day, after the visit to Longbridge, I dropped him off at the end of our private road with instructions how to get to *The Heritage.* I wanted to go on ahead to put lunch on the table as I had invited my Aunt Mary and Cousin, who lived a few hundred yards away, to join us. My Cousin, Bill, saw Harold and went out to greet him. They then walked on together for the rest of the way to *The Heritage*.

At the meal my Aunt passed Harold a glass of home-made wine and said, "Jo gives you this with her love." I had not spoken to either of them of my feelings for Harold because I had not yet fallen for him. The words must have been put into her mouth by the Lord, or she had twigged something between the two of us.

In the afternoon we climbed the Clent Hills and he had *Kim* in harness to help pull him up the hill, so I stopped for breath and described the beautiful views to him before going any higher.

During the course of the evening I discovered I was seven years older than he was. I had invited two friends to join us to hear a tape together before I took Harold home. So our second encounter ended. I wondered what all the spiritual content had done to his views – the Youth for Christ, my address at Longbridge and the tape. I had also read to him my letter from Jesus just before taking him home. In actual fact he had thought that was a better weekend than Attingham Park would have been, and he wanted to express his thanks by giving me a painting.

I prayed on and thanked God for the weekend, knowing that when he shuts some doors he opens others.

**My Mysterious Sickness**

After this I began to have sleepless nights, palpitations, breathlessness and loss of appetite. I had no idea what was wrong with me. I never twigged it was symptoms of falling in love. I decided to take it to the Lord at the following Sunday's Communion Service.

During this time of my sickness and stress, after I had asked, "Why am I sick?" the Lord gave me the following, whose author I forget:

"My Child, I have answered that question before. Why don't you accept my answers and trust me?

My Child, did you not promise me to seek my will in all things? Why then do you start using your own will so soon without asking me for mine first?

My Child, why struggle in your own strength when I have said, 'Do it in mine'?

My Child, why are you faint-hearted and fearful when I have given you my words of encouragement and promises so true?

My Child, have I not shown you that all things work together for good? Leave all to me and you shall be richly blessed.

My Child, I delight in having sweet Communion with you. Why do you communicate so little with me? I want to share your joys and sorrows, sickness and health, the affairs of the world, so that I can make all things well for you.

My Child, have I not promised you rest? If you abide in me more and more you shall know my peace, my rest and quietness.

My Child, think of what I have given for you. I gave my life for you. Cannot you do the same for me?

My Child, why do you rush about? I say, 'Be still and know me.'

My Child, why abide in darkness when I can give you light?

My Child, why lose your way when in me your way is made perfect?

My Child, why search for truth when you can only find the truth in me? Therefore receive me now.

My Child, why do you lack abundant life when you can find this in me?

My Child, obey my voice which is in you. Follow me and my guidance to be led into the paths of righteousness and eternal life of joy and peace for ever.

My Child, let my Spirit have free sway in you and you will be surprised at my power. Take of my Spirit in all its fullness to be to my glory and praise.

My Child, my light will shine forth from you when I am in you for I am the Light of the world, so let it shine.

My Child, serve me and you shall have nothing else to fear and to serve me is to serve him that sent me.

My Child, seek me first and my Kingdom and my gifts will be yours. Why do you not taste and see how good it all is?

My Child, you were born to be my delight. Delight in me and in my word. Keep it and do it.

My Child, my gift of salvation is full and free. Why go on asking for it with your mind and not with all your heart? Take it with repentance and faith, believing it is there for it shall be yours. Be hungry and thirsty and empty of self. Then I will fill you with myself.

At the altar the next Sunday I said, "Lord, I don't believe you want me sick. I'm leaving this problem to you. As I partake of the bread and wine I should like to know the reason for my sickness."

God gave me a number, 464, and I looked it up in Church in the Hymn Book[7]. The hymn was on Holy Matrimony. I said, on finding this, "Who to, Lord?" and I walked home in a daze for I did not know I loved anyone.

**My recovery**

On May 1st, Harold phoned to say he had got a present for me as thanks for a wonderful weekend. I then asked God what I could give to Harold and the answer came, "Yourself." Harold also said he had felt the presence of Jesus and that he wanted to try the Jesus way of life. I asked if he would like to come and stay again when I had my friends Mary and Alec Learmont over to stay on a Healing Mission in the area. He said he would like to come but wouldn't it make a lot of work for me, as he saw how busy I had been the last time. He felt he was in need of prayer since he had felt the presence of evil spirits while in his shed at home. So it was agreed he would come over again. Meanwhile we exchanged tapes, as those, or the telephone, were the only way of communicating as I could not write Braille and he could not read anything else. A sighted person would have to read letters to him so they would not be private.

In this short time I also had more guidance from God. I was on my knees saying, "If you have put it in my heart to marry him you must

---

[7] Ancient and Modern Revised 1st Edition 1950

put it in his heart to marry me. I can't do the proposing. I got up and put the television on. There was someone singing, "Ma, he wants to marry me! Ma, he wants to be my honey bee." That was a good enough answer to me that God had already done it.

All this extra guidance helped to bring me tremendous release from tension and apprehension about being in God's will, and my symptoms were less obvious and disturbing.

I phoned Harold to tell him what God had given me in the hymn at church. We were to purify our lives, refine and purge them to strengthen and beautify each day as the hymn said. (We later chose this Holy Matrimony hymn for our wedding service.)

Harold said on the phone that he had had an attack of the enemy so bad he thought he would not live through the night. His shed felt cold and dark and he felt evil spirits like shadows round about him. My reply was that "God will give his angels charge over you" so that "you will not hurt your foot against a stone."[8] The enemy was angry and knew he was soon to leave their camp territory to enter the Kingdom of God.

## Mary and Alec told about Harold

On Monday May 13th, Mary and Alec arrived to stay with me, and Mary asked, "Who is this boy you have got coming for next weekend?" I told her about Harold. I explained what little I knew, that he was blind, worked as a telephonist, was not yet "born again" and had been involved in occult things. She went to the loo and asked what she was to do about it. She came out saying; "I have got to encourage you to get engaged and to marry on my birthday, 20th September. Don't you think he's the one for you?" I said, "Well, yes, I do, from guidance I've already been given."

At a house meeting in Droitwich in the afternoon of May 13th, when I told Mary and Alec of Harold's recent attack they used the Lord's Prayer, placing Harold's name in the prayer:

"Our Father who art in heaven, hallowed be thy name in Harold,
Thy kingdom come in Harold, Thy will be done in Harold
Lead Harold not into temptation, but deliver Harold from evil.
For Thine is the kingdom and the power and the glory"

This is a most powerful way of praying for anyone. (We did it for Harold's father when he lay dying.)

---

[8] Psalm 91 verses 11 and 12

On May 15th, Mary and Alec were booked to take a healing service in Walsall in the afternoon and to speak at the Guild of Health in Birmingham in the evening. The meeting in Walsall should have been in the church but we were asked to use the hall instead as a couple wanted to get married in the church. Mary said in her talk that we could go forward for proxy healing for someone else in need, so I went forward. As I got out of my seat the wedding bells struck up next door and I thought that was another confirmation.

At the Guild of Health, Mary and Alec were ministering and while they laid hands on me I was given, "Every good gift cometh from the Father above," so I said, "Right, Lord, I'll take him at your word although he's not born again and you say 'do not be unequally yoked'".[9]

This was the night before Harold and I were to meet for the third time.

**Third Meeting with Harold**

I arranged for Harold to travel by bus, and for me to meet him at the bus stop and drive on to *The Heritage* at 2.30 p.m. (Mary and Alec had been invited out to have lunch elsewhere, so this left us free to be together until a meeting at 8.00 p.m. at *The Heritage*.)

I thought that when Harold got off the bus, he would at least squeeze my hand, but, instead, he said, "I declare Divine order and am in Divine order." We drove the short distance home and then he said, "You will find a present for you in my suitcase. It's on the top in a big padded envelope. I went and fetched it and opened the envelope to find a beautiful picture of Christ kneeling at a big black rock called "The Rock of Agony" in the Garden of Gethsemane. It was a book of paintings, entitled "Our Christian Heritage"[10], done by different artists on the life of Christ and there were Bible stories beside the paintings. I was overwhelmed and thought, "How can a blind man see how much I appreciate it, and see my delight at his gift. I decided to show it by going to kiss him for it. He was seated on the sofa, so I bent down and gave him a kiss. He then started kissing me. I said, "Wait a minute. I tell every man to have his first

---

[9] 2 Corinthians 6: 14
[10] Our Christian Heritage, Nelson Beecher Keys and Edward Felix Gallagher, London 1956.

and last kiss unless he is going to marry me." We kissed again. I told him God had told me I was to give myself to him. He said, "Who's doing the proposing, then?" I said, "I haven't a clue!" We were in each other's arms and heaven had taken over the whole affair. He then got down on his knees and proposed. This is what he said.

"My dearest love, I hesitate to speak to you for fear of annoying you. I shudder lest ears other than thine own two dear ones chance to hear this, but the time has come when I must ask you a very serious question, the contemplation of which has caused me many a sleepless night. Will you marry me?"

**Our engagement**

There will never be a proposal like that for anyone else I am sure. We were so happy we decided to go down to the church to say "Thank You" to God for this gift of each to the other, and we sang, "Dear Lord and Father of mankind, forgive our foolish ways" and in walked my cousin Bill, so we told him what had just happened and that he must keep it secret until our parents had been told.

We had just got back to *The Heritage* when Mary and Alec returned. Mary asked, "Has it happened yet?" I said, "Yes". We then had tea together and then the evening people arrived. In the prayer time Mary prayed for us both and our life together so everyone knew if we were going to live together we must be engaged. Then, the next morning, the 17th May, we walked to *The Park,* where my parents lived, to tell them. Mum was in the kitchen and Dad was out in the garden. He came in for his mid-morning drink and said "hello" to us and added, "I'm just going to make my cocoa." I said, "Dad, you'll need something stronger than that. We are engaged!" Dad came across and shook Harold's hand and said, "You don't have to say anything. I know just how you feel." Mum's mouth dropped open with shock after what I had told her about Harold, but she said, "Well, you are old enough now to know your own mind." We stayed only a few minutes longer as we had left Mary and Alec back home.

We had a phone call later from Joan Cameron to say she had arranged a special Communion service for us to be held at St. John's Church, Hagley, by the Reverend T. Doherty. Would we bring family and friends along to celebrate our engagement? So we phoned round and had a wonderful family get together. Harold said,

"Now we are going to be man and wife and to live together, I want all you have got of Jesus so we can be in harmony. Please, take me to the people you went to, to find the truth.

On the Sunday afternoon we went round to tell our friends, and phoned the churchwarden of Crabbs Cross church to ask him to go and tell Harold's parents, as they were not on the telephone. That evening it was arranged that Alec and Mary should talk at the service. I saw Harold's countenance suddenly change and he said he felt as if an octopus was strangling him. I knew it was an attack of the Devil and asked Alec to pray a deliverance prayer and to lay his hands upon Harold. Harold's strength, which had been depleted by the attack, returned.

After the church service a gathering was held at *The Heritage.* By the end of the evening I felt tired so my cousin Bill offered to drive us to take Harold home. It was lovely to be together in each other's arms on the back seat and to relax in each other's company.

The next evening we went to Henley-in-Arden where there was a healing service and we collected Harold to take him along. We allowed a few extra minutes so I could go in to meet his parents for the first time. On leaving I kissed them both goodbyes, never dreaming that that action would be responsible for helping to heal a rift between his father and his sister.

On 21$^{st}$ May a bouquet of flowers fit for the Queen arrived on my doorstep, the first of many more from Harold who sends me them when it's not a birthday or anniversary. Sometimes they arrive after I've been ill or had need of a surprise to cheer me up. (Other husbands please note, it does make a world of difference to be treated like a queen.) I've kept the cards that have been attached to the flowers in a big envelope that is full now after 37 years.

**The Rings**

Harold had gone into Redditch with a friend from the Council to buy me an engagement ring. He asked what sort of ring I would like and I replied, "Anything you choose will suit me." I did not then know what he earned or could afford and I felt sure the Holy Spirit would guide him. I knew for years I would like a sapphire and diamonds, but kept quiet in case those were beyond his means. Jesus in the heart matters more than rings anyway. I learnt later that Harold had stood at a shop window full of rings and that one shone out like a star so he pointed to where the light was and bought it. He had not measured the size of my finger, so took it as it was. He asked his friend what he had pointed his finger at and she told him what it looked like. It had a sapphire in the centre and small diamonds on either side of it. This was another instance of God knowing my heart's desire and showing Harold spiritually how to choose it. He would bring it over the next time we met.

I thought I would like to get a ring made for him. It would be nice, with God's help, to have an individual design with spiritual significance. The caretaker of Broome church worked at a jeweller's shop. He said he could easily get a ring engraved for me if I would just draw the design I wanted. It is a cross upon three steps which represent steps of penitence. Within the cross is a chalice, the cup of suffering. Above the chalice is a dove of peace. Radiating from the cross are rays which represent the light of Christ who is the Light of the World.

The cost of the ring was £42 but it has recently been valued at £250. It is, I think, 18 carat gold. On the inside, beneath the cross, are our initials HNB and JEB and the date 17/06/68, the date when we announced our engagement. We celebrated the purchase of the wedding ring by having a lunch out at *The Dog* at Harvington. Harold was so thrilled with my ring that he said, "I want to give you a pendant with identical design upon it." He had this done and I wore it first on the big day, just to christen it. It also had our initials and the date on the back. I already had a gold chain from a cross I had at my confirmation in 1954. This saved the extra expense of buying a chain.

**Wedding preparations**

Making plans for our wedding and honeymoon in the Lake District kept me busy while continuing my witness for Christ at churches and group meetings. However, all the preparations for the wedding seemed to just flow. Thanks to kind offers of help from my friends everything got done. One friend made the cake, another did the flowers for the bride and bridesmaids and button holes. Yet another friend did the church flowers and two friends took photographs on the day while another taped the service. We listen to this tape on our wedding anniversary and renew our vows. Relations in the printing trade did all the invitation cards and printed the wedding service. Everything turned out to be most professional.

For my wedding dress I chose embossed satin brocade so that Harold could feel the flowers in the design. It cost £25 compared with £1,000 twenty-five years later for my daughter's dress! How time changes things! The bridesmaids were chosen, but two of the four I wanted could not come because the wedding was on a Friday and they had to be at work. The remaining two were Harold's sister and my sister, who had by now returned from America. They wore sapphire blue lace over satin. We decided to keep the colour scheme of flowers in the church to blue and gold. For the wedding cake we chose a guide dog for the top and rings round the sides. My parents came with me to fix the menu and other reception details with the *Worcestershire Hotel,* Droitwich.

Mother arranged for family and friends to have a party at *The Park* on the evening before the wedding. This was far better than stag parties. Harold was to stay with my Aunt Mary and Uncle up the road. They lived within easy walking distance of the church so nothing could go wrong on the day.

**House Hunting for a home for Harold and me**

My parents said if we were to be married we had better start looking for a home. We needed to find one before we fixed a wedding date. Harold knew all the estate agents in Redditch and asked them to send out their lists of available bungalows or houses in the Redditch area. We had no idea of prices and no idea of what we could afford, but started looking round at weekends when he came and stayed with me from after work on Friday night until Sunday night return home. We always took Kim, the guide dog, with us and God used her to help us find the right place. Harold was first given Beethoven's *seventh* symphony on his mind and he said, "We shall know what house is ours on $7^{th}$ June."

We had been going round in hot weather looking for ourselves and we sat in the car, hot and fed up. We said to God, "Father, you have brought us together. Please show us where you want us to live. You must have a house chosen for us somewhere." Then, on $7^{th}$ June, Harold was at work on the Council switchboard. A Mrs. J. Wright phoned. She said, "You sound happy." Harold replied, "Haven't you heard my news? I'm engaged." "Where are you going to live?" she asked. "When we can find a place that isn't a palace or a pig sty," Harold replied. "My step-niece is trying to sell her home privately", she said, "Would you like me to put you in touch?" She told Harold where it was and suggested we look at it on the outside and if we thought we would like it we could see the inside afterwards.

We asked for more signs from the Lord, and he gave them to us as pictures in the moon of things that are on the Redditch coat of arms. One is a fish, as making fishing tackle was then the main industry in Redditch.

We had Alec and Mary with us again and all went to look at the house of which Mrs. Wright had told us, number 43 in a close. The dog went berserk in the car. Harold let her out and she ran to the house below where we had stopped. Then she ran back to Harold and back again to the porch of the house and sat there as if the house was hers already. We four then got out and walked round the house to the back and liked what we saw, so we linked arms round it and claimed it as ours. We had not enough money between us to pay for it, so we left it in God our Father's hands as he is our provider. We then went to *The Elms* at Abberley to have a meal which was both a celebration and also a farewell to Alec and Mary who were returning to their home in Florida.

We then phoned the people who had built and owned number 43, a Mr. and Mrs. Lovegrove. We asked if we could see inside as we were very interested. This was arranged and Harold and I went over on our own to see it. My first impression was of a large lounge in which to hold meetings for the Lord. There were two double bedrooms, a box room or child's bedroom, kitchen, bathroom with separate toilet, and a garage.

We asked if my parents could see it because they would probably have to help us with the money to buy it. This was arranged. Mrs Lovegrove was abroad so Mr. Lovegrove showed my parents round and then we all asked what price he wanted. After some bargaining he and my father agreed on £5,975 which was lower than the first asking price of £6,500. My mother and father had just received a redeemed government bond for £5,795 so they gave it to us as a wedding present. So we would not think that money grew on trees they asked for £8.00 per month interest to be paid back to each of them. This sum was not altered when interest rates changed. We had not paid the price back when they died. Harold's salary was £800 per annum and we lived on £5 per week when we married. Not having to pay a mortgage was a great blessing.

The house was ours by the end of August and we had a few alterations made. The toilet and bathroom were no longer separated but made into a single room. We changed the colour of the paint in the lounge. A hatch was put in the wall between the kitchen and the dining area of the lounge. There was a drop at the back of the house of 5 feet from the veranda to the garden below. This would have been dangerous for Harold so we had a wall built along the outer edge of the veranda. The kitchen door and two French windows in the lounge opened onto this 21 foot wide veranda.

Of course we had to contact solicitors about house purchase. Curtains had to be made or bought for our house. Twenty-one feet of six-foot deep material for lounge curtains cost £28. Now we would pay hundreds of pounds for this. The sign for number 43 was done by a friend who was a sign writer. The name "Fair Haven" was chosen from the Bible. St. Paul's ship, passing along the southern shore of Crete, came to the Fair Haven near the city of Lasea.[11]

**Our Wedding Day and Honeymoon**

Our wedding day, September 20th, dawned sunny, but later a shower of rain wet the roads and pavement. It poured during the service. We had to erect a tent extension as the church held 70 and we had 136 guests. We had the Rectors of Broome and Hagley and the Rural Dean, three ministers, to officiate at the service and the Communion which followed. Seven ministers of different denominations attended as guests. Some came from far. Because of the rain no photographs were taken at the church so we arrived at the *Worcestershire Hotel* a little earlier than we had said. They were not ready for us so some guests went to the bar and some to the lounge while they put the food out. We had asked for finger-sized delicate pastries and sandwiches so people could help themselves and then sit down at small tables in parties. In the end they provided salad with cooked meat and tinned fruit. People had to eat using cutlery and

---

[11] Acts 27: 8

there were not enough seats or tables. Mother was in tears over it all and she and Dad went back to complain and got a good refund. I was radiantly happy regardless of circumstances. The weather cleared up and photographs were taken outside in the garden. We changed at 4.30 p.m. and left at 5.15 p.m., being chauffeur driven to *The Fair Haven,* our new home, where we spent our first night.

Arrangements had to be made with Guide Dogs for the Blind at Leamington for Kim, Harold's dog, to be cared for during our honeymoon. She was taken there on the afternoon before our wedding day.

After breakfast the next morning we set off for the honeymoon, calling at *The Park* on the way. Guests there were still discussing the wedding and there were more presents to open which had been left at *The Worcestershire.* We had a good journey to the Red House Hotel, Keswick. The landlords there were very disappointed not to have Kim as a guest because I had asked if they would accept her when I did the booking, but we changed our minds about taking her.

We had very mixed weather with quite a lot of rain but we managed to get out and about most days and got some lovely slides by which to remember it.

On our first night we had only been in bed a short while when there was a knock at the door. Could the manager and another man come in to get up in the loft above us as there was something wrong with the water system? We said, "Yes" so it was sorted out.

We were glad to have a private bathroom off our bedroom as one day we decided to climb up the hill behind the hotel to get a better view of the lake below. We had got half way up when Harold slipped and fell into the mud and sheep muck. At a style he said he wanted to go back for a bath and change of clothes, so we never got the hill-top photograph for which we had set out. Harold looked so awful I had to go ahead to see if the pathway to the hotel and to our bedroom was clear so no one would see us.

One evening we were travelling homewards towards the hotel. Harold was thinking about the choice of menu and what he would like when I shouted, "Darling, the sunset over Rydal water looks like a pot of gold. I must get a picture of it. I parked the car and ran quickly to the spot from which I saw it. I took a picture but by then the light was poor and it did not turn out well. Harold said, "Darling, I thought our honeymoon was going to be *in* camera not *on* camera."

I used him as a point of interest in several shots and made him sit and wait for the sun to come out or for clouds to change so that I could compose a better picture.

All good things have to come to an end and our journey home was a long one. We took a packed lunch from the hotel instead of stopping at a pub or restaurant.

Kim, Harold's guide dog, was delighted to see us after the honeymoon was over and continued working for three years from our engagement.

**Thanksgiving on the New Year's Eve**

This was my prayer of thanksgiving at the end of 1968, the year of our marriage. "Thank you, Father, for a year full of light and love and for the many new adjustments made by your help and grace. I have done less for you and more for myself. I have spent less time in prayer and devotion and praise yet there has been so much more for which to praise you. Times of abiding produced little new knowledge, yet struggles with the enemy occurred more often though there were some victories won. My questioning doubts and disturbances show lack of faith on my part. There have been fewer times of healing and of hearing you speak and feeling your presence, yet we, your children, must grow up. You are leading me onward and upward by experiences and by trust in you. I have a new life, a new home, new friends, new adventures and missionary work. 'The hopes and fears of all the years are met in you tonight.' You have answered so many prayers and all your gifts and promises have been fulfilled in marriage and safe journeys over many miles and in the kindness of others and all our comforts of food, clothing, a warm home and family. We are truly grateful for the joys and tears which are a part of life, for your presence at all times, for promises claimed and healing received, for opportunities used, witness given, spiritual refreshing and the abundant supply from your store.

I resolve to show more devotion, trust, obedience, faithfulness, surrender, service to fellow men, and more use of time and talents to advance the Kingdom. These cannot be done by my own strength, will, or effort. They are only possible with your help, grace, support and strength. AMEN."

## CHAPTER FIVE: GROWTH AFTER BEING BORN AGAIN

When I knew my calling I asked Jesus to take everything the Devil had used in me, or through me, and replace them with his Holy Spirit's control and the Holy Spirit's gifts and fruits. I have never had the temptation to go back to the ways of "the Old D". Jesus' way is so much more wonderful and I renounced my partaking of occult things in my past and cut off my ancestral connections with it. I did blame my maternal grandfather for starting the rot, the "sins of the fathers being visited unto the third and fourth generation"[12]. Years later on at a crusade at Malvern I was shown this blaming was wrong and that we all have the choice to do good or evil. I went for counselling on this subject and was prayed for. I'm very glad I kept a notebook and diary so I can refer back to them and refresh my memory. It is 39 years ago that this all happened, but so much more has happened since that I hardly know where to begin. I had so much to learn and unlearn that it was quite confusing at the start. I was involved in reading the Bible going to conferences, reading books, meeting other believers, listening to tapes, watching others already in the ministry and having ministers to stay and show me the ropes. They came from many parts of the world – Australia, Sweden, India, and Guyana.

### Full Immersion Baptism

The day after I returned from Lee Abbey, I went for evening service at Chawn Hill Four Square Baptist Church, and learnt that there was to be a baptismal service afterwards. It took half an hour to fill the pool, so to occupy the time as it was my first visit and I didn't know anyone, I read a book from the bookstall.

Since I had never witnessed a full immersion baptism, I was interested to see what went on. As the service progressed I realised it was something I should do for myself. After all, Jesus gave the example so it must be right. I wondered how I could be baptised in this way in an Anglican church and did not know the answer. So I prayed, "Lord, this is what I want to do, but how?" After the last person had been immersed, Mr. Meek, who was the preacher, said, "The Holy Spirit has told me there is someone here who wants to be baptised. If they like to come forward we have some clothes they can borrow." I shot out of my seat and went up to the front and a

---

[12] Exodus 20: 4

lady took me through to a changing room where I undressed and put on the white overall they provided and took a towel and went back to be baptised. Mr. Meek asked if I knew the Lord and I said "Yes". He had a baptismal verse for me "Be strong and of a good courage. Fear not for the Lord thy God doth go with thee. He will not fail thee or forsake thee."[13]

People came to congratulate me and offer a cup of tea when I was dressed again. They asked me how I had given my life to Jesus. I told them, and this led to many invitations to go to speak to groups in the area. More doors opened for me to testify and witness in service for the Master.

It was with great trepidation that I went to see our then Rector, the Rev. Charles Marsh, who had asked by phone if I would go to see him. He did not say what he wanted to see me about. However, when, in my spiritualist days, I had gone to ask if I could pray for him he was not best pleased, to put it mildly! So, fearful of what was coming, I sat at the rectory gate praying and remembering how hurt and frightened I had been at the last encounter. He had every right to have reacted the way he did, but I did not then have the understanding to know the wrong in that method. But all that had changed through my knowing Jesus. I thought he would not understand the change that had happened to me. I was willing to face the music, but when God asks you to do a job he goes ahead and prepares the way. You could have knocked me down with a feather when he said, "I have heard of all the good you have been doing in the parish in my absence through illness. I want to anoint you and give you a blessing to continue the work of visiting the sick, giving prayer and the laying on of hands and starting the tape group and so on. There was only one thing he was sorry about, namely that I had succumbed to full immersion baptism, but, as I had not been prepared beforehand, it did not count and therefore it did not annul my membership of the Church of England.

I heard of Chawn Hill and went to see what they did – coffee clubs, other meetings and services. I was very impressed with their love, friendship and Bible teaching. I told my cousin Bill about them and

---

[13] Deuteronomy 31: 6

he went along and was converted there himself. He lived just up the road from me, so we and six other Born Again Christians in the parish started meeting together. What an answer to our prayers for other conversions!

## Harold's Chawn Hill Baptism

Much later, my fiancé, Harold, wanted to have the same experiences of Jesus that I had had. His request was fulfilled at the same place with the same people.

Harold requested full immersion baptism by Mr. Meek at Chawn Hill, but when Mr Meek interviewed Harold he told him he was not ready for it. Early in the same week, the Woods had asked the Reverend Grimshaw to speak again at their house group and they invited us to go along. I was already booked to attend a British and Foreign Bible Society meeting in Stourbridge, but I agreed to drop Harold off on my way and to collect him later.

On June 30th he was baptised as he had hoped he would be. When he told his parents they said, "What do you want a second baptism for? You've been done as a child." Jesus was baptised when he had no need to be, but he wanted to be an example for believers to follow for the years that remain until his return. Baptism does not give you entrance to eternal life. Only Jesus can do that by his death on the cross and by his Spirit. There is no biblical example of someone else's faith and promises being used to get you to eternity. Each individual has to respond to Jesus to make him Lord of their lives to have eternal life.

While these important steps were being taken Harold was at work Mondays to Fridays and I was out and about doing the Lord's work.

## Progress in the Christian Life

In 1967 before my marriage, I attended a conference at a College in Birmingham on healing ministry. I gave six talks during the year about The Holy Land and eleven talks on the healing ministry. I visited fourteen people to give help of one kind or another, had two house groups, one at my home, *The Heritage,* and one at my parents' home, *The Park.* There was also a tape group meeting in the village. I attended church Synods and meetings of the British and Foreign Bible Society. I was in the church choir and went to regular meetings of Youth for Christ and the Guild of Health and attended the Photographic Society and Women's Institute meetings. I judged the W.I. cookery and preservation sections in village shows. I worked for my parents and ran my own home. All this contrasted with my pre-born again days when I had little faith or knowledge of Jesus, and I sat alone in deep depression doing nothing to help anybody and going nowhere.

**The Gift of Speaking in Tongues**

In November 1966 I went to the conference centre at Swanwick, Derbyshire, to take the parents of a child who had died in August. It was only a weekend course, but this led me to meet someone who would invite me to hear a talk at his home. When the speaker had finished he invited those present to go for healing and baptism in the Spirit, speaking in tongues. I did not go forward, for I was afraid of being taken over by the Holy Spirit after being taken over by demon spirits in the past. I had not learnt enough about it either, so I bought books on the subject. It was a long time before I received it in the lounge at home after my marriage.

On another occasion, before Harold and I were married, I had arranged a weekend at a guest house in Blackpool at which the Reverend Stan Woods was to be the speaker. Some of his parishioners came along as well. We occupied the whole guest house. It seemed a good idea because there were so many newborn Christians in my home village of Broome who needed teaching on the Holy Spirit and further instruction in the faith. The Lord put his hand and Spirit upon the event, and one evening all those who were sitting chatting on the staircase received the baptism of the Holy Spirit and were speaking in tongues.

I was very tired and not then ready to let myself go to the Holy Spirit, so I went to bed. Next morning I was so disturbed that I went out early and walked on the sands along the sea front. I sat down and seagulls suddenly came swirling round my head. They gave their seagull cries in loud unison. I felt they were speaking the tongues I could not speak. This brought me relief for a while. I shall never forget it. I reckoned it was my past beliefs in other spirits that had to be dealt with more fully if I were to have the Holy Spirit's gift of tongues.

It happened in January 1969 while we were in the lounge at home. Harold said, "Speak out what the Spirit is giving you." I mumbled what I thought sounded gibberish and I wanted to see if the words were in the Bible. It came out as, "God is true"[14], so I doubted no more. With use it developed and I enjoyed singing in tongues while driving the car, and at times for praise and worship or when praying for the sick. Harold has the gift of interpretation which he uses for my tongue when we pray together. In the same year I was licensed to administer the chalice at Holy Communion.

## The Ashram

We heard of a Christian Ashram to be run in Wales by Dr. E. Stanley Jones. We were a bit suspicious from the title and made some enquiries before booking.

We learnt much that was new to us on the Ashram on prayer and meditation and sharing in time of the overflowing heart. We took part in the continuous prayer chain that went on day and night throughout the whole convention of four days and four nights. We were taught some new graces to say at meal times and we enjoyed walks in the countryside in our free time.

It was here that I had a small fainting turn because I was by now four months pregnant. I had been in the prayer room during the night and felt sickly standing for some time early in the morning. Fresh air and a drink of water soon put me right.

While at the Ashram we met a Swedish minister, Sten Nielson, who said he would be pleased to stay with us and give talks about healing. While he was with us Harold had a bad red rash that came up on his neck. It irritated him and creams did not help. He asked for prayer and Sten said, "What's irritating you at work?" Harold was irritated when certain people wanted priority over others, to be given their phone numbers immediately instead of waiting their turn. Sten told him that his inward irritation was expressing itself in the rash and that if he could stop his inner reaction the rash would go, which it did.

## Assemblies of God

A lady from the Assembly of God Church invited me to speak at a ladies' meeting held at Bates Hill Methodist Church. I was very impressed by the joyful and interested crowd of people there. They were very friendly and came to speak to me over cups of tea. One asked if I would be prepared to speak and give my testimony at her

---

[14] 2 Corinthians 1: 18

ladies' meeting at the Assembly of God Church in Redditch. I agreed so a date was fixed. This made me think God had a plan for us to attend that church. We went along to see what they did and how they ran their meetings. It was the first time we had experienced the Holy Spirit's gifts in operation in a service. The clapping of hands and the long time spent in singing choruses were quite new to us Anglicans. It started us attending their church regularly though we never became members of it.

However, at one meeting of the church an elderly lady tapped me on the shoulder and said, "You live in Astwood Bank, don't you?" I said we did and so did she. Her name was Gertie Street. Since that first meeting we saw a lot of each other. In fact she became our baby sitter and came into our lives many more times. She lived to be a hundred years and seven months old.

The minister we first met at that church soon left for Canada and another one arrived. Pastor Tom Jones with his wife became real friends and we had many wonderful times being taught deeper truth by him. In fact he dedicated our daughter at that church after she was born. I was asked to show my Holy Land slides there and at other meetings in the area as word spread around. Harold was also asked to speak for the Guide dogs for the Blind Association. Bookings came for us to go to schools, church groups and fellowships and even dog clubs.

# CHAPTER SIX: OUR DAUGHTER'S BIRTH AND CHILDHOOD

Friends and relations were having babies and I began to feel like the Biblical Hannah who desired a child. My desire grew stronger and prayers for this desire to be fulfilled were said more often.

One evening we went to the Assembly of God Church in Redditch and I went forward to the altar for the laying on of hands for my heart's desire. The Rev. Tom Jones was ministering and when he asked what I wanted I said, "A baby". The lady in the healing line next to me said, "I know you are going to have a baby. I have just felt it leap in my womb." She had been married twice but was childless so how did she know what it was like unless the Holy Spirit revealed it to her then by an actual feeling in her womb? When I returned to my seat I looked at the painting on the wall behind the altar. It was a mural of a shepherd and sheep at sunset and the words "Jesus Christ, the same yesterday, today and forever"[15]. Then I had a revelation. In the very centre of the sun's rays in the picture was a tiny foetus. I had not seen it before. I went to the doctor, but he said it was too early to test. I should return in two to three months. In late February, I had a missed period. If this was the first sign a miracle had happened at the altar rail in Redditch. As there was no sign of any trouble we continued with speaking engagements as before.

As I was a speaker for the Mothers' Union I went to one of their retreats, and was greatly blessed by attending it. I came across some advice written in a missionary magazine which fitted my situation. Part of it ran as follows:

> "My child, it is not necessary for you to know much to please me. It is sufficient to love much....Speak to me as you would to a mother if she drew thee near to her.....Dost thou dread something painful?.....Is there in thine heart a vain fear which is not reasonable, but which is tormenting thee?.....Trust thyself wholly to my care. I am here. I see everything. I will not leave thee."[16]

---

[15] Hebrews 13: 8

[16] "India's Women: The Magazine of the Church of England Zenana Missionary Society, Vol. III, Jan Feb. Patterson Press, 1883

The old Devil had already been making me fearful of the pain of childbirth and this just put my mind at rest and peace on this matter. I knew what my mother had suffered at age 36 when she had my sister and age 38 when she had me and I was 40. Old wives tales tell of the worst that can happen to an older Mum. Even my doctor said I could not have a home birth as there might be complications at my age and a theatre might be necessary in an emergency. This was a prophetic word from the Lord but I did not take it in or believe it at the time.

**Predictions concerning my future baby**

My cousin Kate and her husband and youngest son, with whom I had stayed in Canada when I was 25, came to England. Kate was mother to three boys and said she was sure I was going to have a boy as she saw the signs. Another friend thought I would have a son. I thought that the law of averages would say a son, as Harold's parents had had 4 boys and a girl and these produced 8 granddaughters. My parents had had 2 girls so deserved a grandson. We did not have scans in those days to reveal the sex beforehand. I did some knitting in blue and white wools but my baby proved to be allergic to wool so I gave the clothes away.

In July I felt the quickening.

**Toxaemia**

After we had been witnessing in Bath, I drove home and noticed, when I got there, that my ankles were very swollen. Over the garden fence I saw my neighbour. She had 3 children and had told me to have a chat with her if ever I was worried about anything. So I told her about my ankles and she said I should see my doctor. So, at 4.00 p.m., I walked up to the surgery and my doctor did a thorough examination. He said, "Your blood pressure is dangerously high and you have toxaemia, living too well!" I was to go home and straight to bed where I was to stay for a week. I was not to cook for my husband and his friend. They would have to get a pub meal instead that evening.

On the way home from the doctor's I passed a friend's house so I called in to ask her to pray for me. She offered to help and so did my neighbour. My parents said they would come over next day and plan how to manage for the week. No one then knew that the week would be extended to four months, though I was allowed to do an evening meal and to attend pregnancy classes once a month.

Someone living up the road lost her baby through a miscarriage. I saw her being taken away in an ambulance. I therefore asked the Lord in prayer what my condition was all about and would I lose my baby. He gave me a verse from scripture, "See that ye be not troubled for all these things must come to pass but the end is not yet."[17] I knew by this that there would be a battle with the enemy, but I would not lose the baby. God said he would supply all my needs and he did.

Harold had a telephone and adjustable lamp installed by the bed and my mother brought over a commode. The doctor said the complete rest had led to an improvement in my blood pressure but I was still not to do much. I could do an evening meal provided I sat at a high stool we had been given. The enforced rest gave me time for Bible study, reading and knitting.

The Church of England minister, the Rev. Rhodes, came faithfully every week to give me Communion. He smoked a pipe and talked of cricket. The Church of the Assembly of God prayed for me throughout my pregnancy and delivery and afterwards. I could feel support from another prayer chain as well as from family and friends.

As time went on and the baby grew I suffered from extremely painful piles. This was not a passing phase but lasted for months. Ice packs, ointments and bathing in cold water were of little help. I came to dread going to the toilet. At the age of 21 I had had an operation for haemorrhoids at the Queen Elizabeth hospital in Birmingham but the effect was not long-lasting. They soon came back and were troublesome. I learnt that constipation is one of the side effects of pregnancy because of pressure of the baby on the bowel.

As full term drew nearer I wondered how I would cope with the effort of labour. I wanted to experience it, but not the prolonged pain. Mother wanted me to have a Caesarean operation privately but

---

[17] Matthew 24: 6

I felt the National Health Service was where God wanted me to be. He had said that he was going to use me as a witness before the doctors and nurses. He gave me a verse that showed that trouble lay ahead. It was, "The enemy will come in like a flood, but I will raise my standard against him."[18]   I went round the hospital at Bromsgrove with the pre-natal class and when we got to the theatre I just knew I would be in there and that drama would ensue.

The family all came up trumps. Diana, my sister, would take me to hospital and look after Harold. Mother would come after the birth to look after the three of us. The doctor had said I could apply for a home help three days a week and the health visitor would call. A child clinic was held in the Church Hall for further help and advice when the baby's weight would be recorded and inoculations given.

Usually toxaemia babies come early and are under weight because they cannot draw full nourishment from the womb. They can also be still born if the correct care is not given.

Our baby was due on November 27th and as that date approached we discussed names for the child. I picked boys' names – John after my father, Richard after my grandfather, but Harold said that God had told him that it was a girl and that she must be called Abigail. No one in either family had this name and it was not one we would have thought of if left to ourselves.   I had bought all the birth announcement cards and filled in the addressees. I left Mother to complete them with the date of birth, weight, and name of the child. When the time came she did a shortened form, "Gail". My sister said she would be nicknamed "Windy-bags" at school. She was later called Gale which got shortened to Gay until that word was used for homosexuals and she asked to be called "Abi" instead.

**My confinement**

The baby did not put in an appearance on 27th November so they told me to go in on Monday 30th after a weekend at home. My sister took me in and I was taken to a small side room in the maternity wing. Two nurses were making up the bed for me. One suggested that I should be put somewhere else but the other said, "Oh, let her stay here!" This matter was decided by God for a special reason that

---

[18] Isaiah 59: 19

would become apparent later. On the bedside cabinet I noticed a piece of yellow paper which said that a certain doctor would be arriving for his first day at the hospital. I should not have seen this but it did not bother me as I knew God was in charge of everything anyway. The nurse told me to get undressed, go along to the preparation room and return to this side room afterwards.

I was then taken up to the theatre I had seen on my visit to the hospital. Two doctors were waiting for me there to have the waters broken to try to induce labour. Labour did not start that day so I was strung up on the couch with my legs in a position to allow them to break the membrane. The doctor tried to do this three times unsuccessfully, whereupon I said out loud in front of them all, "Please Jesus, will you help me." They went off to confer in a small room. When they came back they said I had got my dates mixed up. The baby had not dropped down fully and I had better go back to my room. The nurse accompanied me and Jesus then answered my prayer as the waters broke as I was walking back. I said to her, "There you are, you see what the doctors could not do Jesus has done." She said, "It's a good job he has, for they did not know what to do with you if he hadn't." She left me with the pads to absorb the waters and hopefully start labour.

I praised the Lord, read my Bible, and waited and waited for labour to begin. I was told not to get out of bed for it could lead to trouble. Lunch came and I ate well, thinking I would need a good supply of energy.

After lunch a nurse came in and said, "You're Mrs. Bagby aren't you?" I said I was. She said that a lady called Jean Bendall had written to her to tell her to look out for me. Her name was Muriel Banks. She was a Pentecostal Christian and believed like I did, so we had a great time of fellowship together. I asked if she would kindly phone my husband to say that nothing had started, yet all was well, and would he continue to pray. She left and went back on duty. All the links were falling into place as God was working things out through Lee Abbey, Jean Bendall and Muriel. I had wanted Christians to be at the birth so we could really share God's gift to us together. The evening and night came and I was kept awake by noises down the corridor of others having their babies. Their screams and moans did not help me as I was thinking I would be next. Nothing happened until next morning when doctors did their rounds and it was decided at 11.00 a.m. to put me onto a drip that would start labour artificially. Lunch came and again I ate well thinking of the energy that would be needed. It was after 2.00 p.m. when I felt the first twinge of pain. Nurses came and went, doing various checks on the baby and myself.

Muriel came in to say God had given her a word for me. I said, I guessed it was the same that he had given to me, "The enemy will come in like a flood, but I will raise my standard against him." She said it was. After she went, the labour pains continued to increase. In my spirit I knew all was not well by 5.15 p.m. so I asked the nurse to do another check up on us both. She went and later came back with a sister who listened to the baby. She left and came back with two doctors who examined me and said, "Mrs. Bagby, you are not opening up properly and it is stressing the baby and we can feel the baby is the wrong way round, brow presentation." They then set up a sonar scope to see what was going on in the womb. This machine made a high pitched ping-ping noise and one could see the distress the baby was in. They decided I must be rushed off to the theatre for a Caesarean. I said I would like my minister to pray over me before the operation. They asked where he lived. When I said "Worcester" they said there was no time left to get him. I looked at the open door and there he was at reception asking after me. I called, "Hey, Pastor, I'm here. Come and pray for me." He came in and the nurses who had been preparing me for the operation left. I was still groaning in labour though the drip had been removed. Pastor said a prayer and told me he was on his way to the church and they would all be praying for a safe delivery. He left and I was wheeled down to the theatre. It was now 7.00 p.m.

Unknown to me, Harold had arrived in a taxi with Angus who was a Christian. They were told to wait as I was on my way to the theatre. Going down the corridor I shut my eyes so did not see Mr. Hudson, a man from the Assembly of God Church who had been visiting his wife. He recognised me and decided to wait to learn the result before going on to the church. I asked the doctor if I could have the anaesthetic by injection rather than a mask but he said that a mask was safer for the baby's sake.

70

I came round in the ward I had been in before. All the Christians were round me – Harold, Angus, Mr. Hudson and Muriel. (Muriel, then off duty, and hearing of my plight, had asked if she could be with me in the theatre and help with the delivery.) All I could say was, "Oh my poor tummy! The Christians around me were saying, "You have a lovely baby daughter!" I drifted in and out of consciousness, but saw a nurse with a white bundle in the doorway. Harold was saying, "Coo-ee, Abigail darling!" Muriel gave me a tablet for the pain and all left quickly.

(Abigail weighed 6 pounds and 13 ounces at birth. She was covered with a lot of fuzzy hair on her neck and shoulders. She had great folds of skin in wrinkles which made her look old and wizened. From the position and pressures in the womb her head had been squashed into the shape of a question mark. She was not able to hold it up until she was a year old.)

The next thing I knew was a nurse coming in who said, "Just look how they have left this poor woman!" I had been very sick in my sleep. Two nurses changed the sheets and then asked if I would like to see my daughter. She was brought in and gave me the biggest smile. I said, "Jesus is Lord and I give you back to him." I did not realise that what I had said was the same as Hannah, in the Bible, said about Samuel her son[19]. Abigail was taken back to the nursery until feeding time.

Before Abigail was 24 hours old the doctors asked permission to give her a tuberculosis injection because of Harold's former illness with tubercular meningitis. I thought the injection would be in her arm. I was not told it would be in her spine. It was done, but it caused future problems. She suffered terrible cramps in her legs when doing exercises and before she could talk she used to scream and we did not know why until an osteopath said she had obtrusions from it.

**Recovery**

It was December 1970 and there were electricity cuts. We were told to stay in our beds and babies would be brought to us. I started to breast feed my baby and thought "She's not interested in feeding." In the semi-darkness I looked at the name tag on the baby's wrist. It

---

[19] Samuel 1: 28

71

was "Gibbs". I shouted, "Nurse, I've been given the wrong baby!" She took the baby away and brought Abigail, telling me to wash my own nipples and hands. Poor Abi sucked and sucked and only got half an ounce of milk at a time. The milk was not coming so they gave me hormones to produce more. There was no result so they gave me more hormones to stop the milk. You can imagine what my body felt like. I had lost 2 stone in weight and had muck sweats and a hundred other things as well. They said I could stay in the side ward until another Caesarean operation came along. Then I would be moved into the main ward, but God kept me in the private side ward by holding back all the other babies that were due in those eleven days.

There was a time when after the birth the shock came out. I awoke one night, shaking uncontrollably, and rang the bell. No one came. I rang it again and a cleaner came in and told me there was a shortage of nurses as babies were being delivered but she would see what she could do. A nurse came in with a blood pressure gauge, then another nurse, then a sister. I learnt later the pressure was so high I should have had fits and convulsions but I was given a drink of milk and a sleeping pill and all was normal again. I told Harold next day that I thought I was going to die and to get more prayer which he did, bless him.

It was my 41$^{st}$ birthday five days after the birth so my side ward was filled not only with birth congratulations but also with birthday greetings. My parents came one day and left a casserole dish of cooked pheasant for my sister to collect when she brought Harold to see me. Fog came down and I feared they might not make it and that the pheasant under the bed would start to smell but they did come so all was well.

Nurses would come for a chat when they had a spare moment, especially at night because they all sensed peace and calm in the presence of Jesus. I was able to witness to them quite freely and those who had faith or were searching opened up to spiritual things. When the doctor who had operated on me came round on his morning visits he said what a good job he had done and how well it was healing. I said it was because Jesus had laid his hands upon him and I had laid my hands on the wound and blessed it daily ever since that day.

The lady whose baby I had mistakenly been given had an abscess on her wound and it would not heal. Concern was growing about this complication. I said in my case the difference was when Jesus was put in charge. They did not count on God being present in time of trouble as I had done.

On 10th December Harold had the day off work. Father drove Mother over to our house and Angus drove Harold to the hospital to collect Abigail and me.

Abi was a very contented baby in the nursery. She did not show any signs of the anaesthetic and she did not cry. She made up for that later!

**At Home following Abi's birth**

We did not know how Harold's dog, Kim, would react to the new arrival so we shut her in the kitchen until Abi had been put into the nursery and I was in bed. Then Kim was allowed to say, "Hello". She was obviously pleased to have me home and showed no sign of jealousy.

Following eleven days of seclusion in a small ward I found everything very noisy and traffic seemed to be going at great speed. I was glad to get back into bed and to adjust to the new routine. All I did was bath and feed Abi and bathe myself. I was so weak that I tired easily and I had nightmares and muck sweats in the night. Mother thought I should see the doctor and wanted to be with me in the bedroom when he came. However, he sent her packing and told me I must pull myself together. I had two children to look after now and I must not linger in bed any longer. He gave me some pills to make me sleep and left. The pills made me doped and fit for nothing so I put them down the toilet. They were better than any toilet cleaner I had ever used so what they would have done to me I do not know!

Christmas came and went and mother had knocked herself up doing too much. She caught a bad cold and felt she must return home and take to her bed herself. Diana, my sister told me later how very ill mother had been.

When I went for the six-week check up with the gynaecologist he said, "Mrs. Bagby, do you realise how lucky you are to have your daughter alive?" I said, "Luck does not play a part in my life." I told him God had given her to us by prayer and the laying on of hands. A church and others had prayed for me all through the pregnancy and delivery. God was in charge of my life anyway. Apparently I was the talk of that hospital for two years afterwards. (Some years later the hospital was closed.)

First walk outdoors

I remember the first day I went out, pushing the pram for a little way just up the street. People asked me where I got the baby from as she seemed to them an instant arrival. They had not seen me showing any signs of pregnancy because I had been indoors for six months. They had not been prepared to see a pram and a baby.

I had post natal depression for a few weeks when I was left to fend for myself again. I remember when washing nappies I had to use milk bottle tops to count the number of rinses I had given them. I hated having to decide anything, even what clothes to put on Abi. As it was winter I used to put her in the pram in the porch which is mostly glass and gets quite warm if the sun is out, but can be cold if there is no sun. Once when I went to collect her from the porch for her feed I found she did not respond to my talking to her. I went round to my neighbour and she said she thought the baby was cold. She rubbed her to get the circulation going again and all was well. Another little scare I had when she was tiny was that while she was feeding she went bright red and her eyes rolled. I thought the teat had had too big a hole and that she had got wind. I spoke in tongues and held her up to pat up the wind and all was well.

**Dedication of Abi to God and her Christening**

On February 7th 1971 Abi was dedicated at the Assembly of God Church in Redditch. There was a prophecy over her by the Revd. T. Jones who said God had great plans for her life and that is why the enemy had come in like a flood and tried to kill her before birth and at birth. The congregation promised to pray for her.

The Rev. Rhodes came to see us about baptism. He was chatting away when Abi started crying. He said, "Oh, let her cry. It won't hurt. I put all my kids at the far end of the house and let them cry. You can pamper them too much." Abi went on crying, but I thought I had better obey the clergyman so I did not go to her until he left ten minutes later. She had pulled her little cardigan over her face and

74

scratched her eczema until it was bleeding. I shouted to Harold, "I'll never take his advice again. Look what a state she's in! I wish I had followed my own instinct to go to her." This reaction made her afraid of blood. How careful we have to be over our reactions!

To keep people happy, Abi was christened on April 18th at the church of St. Matthias and St George, Astwood Bank. There was a party for Godparents, family and friends afterwards. Abi cried throughout the service and nothing could distract her.

**Abi's Eczema and early fears**

When she was in the pram in the hall I left her under a painting I had done of a circus horse in a ring under the spotlight. It was all in black and white and the horse was dappled grey with white mane and tail. When she woke she looked up, saw the painting and screamed. She looked fearful and distressed at seeing it. I realised that in her mind it reminded her of the theatre light and stress when she was born. The fear came back in a flash. I removed the painting and all was calm in the hall.

Her eczema started at five months of age with a few spots and a rash on her face. The doctor this could be a long-lasting condition, but he gave me a tube of cream to use sparingly on the blotches on her face. He also said I should try goats' milk instead of cows' milk and try a different brand of baby food. (Unfortunately the changes just caused her to become difficult over food.) I should use mild soap to wash her and give her oatmeal baths and long soaks in oils. Her clothes should be washed in "Lux" soap flakes. These were only a temporary help. The eczema just spread all over her body and we tried everything, even honey and sulphur and Stockholm tar. We bandaged her hands and arms to prevent her scratching, making scabs which had to be soaked and peeled off by degrees. Before she was a year old she suffered asthma attacks and hay fever. We tried medication, steaming kettles, coal tar, burning night lights, ionisers, air fresheners and filters. She had tests to find out allergies. They proved that walnuts could kill her and she was also allergic to dairy products, eggs, white flour, colourings in drinks, and flavourings in crisps. When she was older she helped to make cakes. If she licked a spoon the eczema came up all round her mouth where the spoon and its contents had touched her face. Cats and dogs also caused great distress so living with a guide dog was far from ideal. Paint made her vomit for hours until we realised what was the cause and took her away from the house.

When she was one year old I went to see an endocrinologist in Birmingham in the hope that he might be able to aid the restoration of my husband's sight. His diagnosis was that both Harold and I had a glandular dysfunction for which he prescribed treatment. We also asked about Abigail who had the same dysfunction inherited from both of us. He said she was too young to receive treatment. More would be known about her make-up by the time she was four or five years of age. This was helpful for the long run. Our treatment and later hers, is described in another chapter.

As she grew older people told us to try this, that, and the other creams for her eczema – even honey because it contained pollen to which she might be allergic! She should avoid chocolate, oranges, nuts, and things that warm the blood. She should not have white flour or sugar. "Have you tried goat's milk?" Yes, we had. Then a specialist from Harley Street, London, told us to keep her from eating anything from an animal, and crisps and soft drinks that contained a certain colouring substance. Eczema is a terrible itch to contend with and for six years I slept on a 2'6" bed to hold her in my arms to prevent scratching which caused even greater problems of weeping and formation of crusty scabs. These caused more itching and the whole process would start again. I bandaged the full length of her arms and put mittens on her hands. If she was not watched she would soon get the mittens off. I used to get meals ready with one hand whilst holding her on my hip with the other hand so that she could not start rubbing herself on the furniture.

**Fear of noises and of water**

Ever since Abi was a very tiny baby she had been afraid of noises. This made her fearful of going out in the garden or the street alone. She would cover her ears with her hands and run to the inside of pavements at the sound f traffic. She could not stand the sound of such things as an egg beater, the vacuum cleaner, the or loud sneezing. I could link these fears to sounds she may have heard while still in the womb, when I had ultra sound scans and when our house was treated with cavity wall insulation.

She was also terrified by a squeaky noise made when I opened up a wooden clothes horse on which to hang laundry. She was also afraid of aeroplanes, having been on my lap when a baby, while we were watching the news. Prince William of Gloucester's plane crashed and caught fire. We reacted with "Oh dear!" in a changed tone of voice which she heard. She could also see the great cloud of smoke rising from the plane. She called a plane, "Tiss". If I told her to go out to play in the garden she would ask, "Will there be a Tiss, Mummy?" If a plane did fly over she would put her hands over her ears and run into the house.

She was healed of these fears when she was about three years and three months old, thanks to the ministry of a Christian friend.

However, before she was five, she slipped in the bath and fell face downwards. My quick reaction of picking her up before she drowned caused her to have a fear of the bath. As she would not get in, I started to stand her on a cork mat and give her a flannel bath. Our neighbour was outside one day with her three children. They were playing in a paddling pool for it was a warm summer day. The neighbour suggested that Abi might lose her fear of the bath if I took her round to play in the paddling pool with the other children. Abi did let me bathe her in the bath after that but she still hated getting her face wet. This caused problems when her secondary boarding school took her to swimming baths. She picked up verruca there and missed a whole term of swimming because of them. It was not until years later that she learnt to swim at a leisure centre.

**Abi's illnesses**

By the time Abi was two and a half, she was often ill with fevers, tonsillitis, influenza, and bronchitis. We were advised to see a Christian doctor in Worcester who treated patients with prayer for healing and with homeopathic medicine. His name was Dr. Calcott, and he was a very loving, kind, understanding and sympathetic man whose house church we later joined. He prescribed tablets that we used that were slightly beneficial. He also asked us if we would like to attend his house church where a fellowship lunch was provided by different mothers in turn and where there was a crèche so that the parents could worship in freedom. We became members for a number of years of his house church fellowship. It happened like this: because there was no Sunday school at the nearest Church of England, I took Abigail to the Baptist Church, while Harold and the dog continued to go to the Church of England. This separation could have made an opening for the Old Devil to try to break up our marriage, so when we were invited to the house church we could all go together. However it was nearly 40 miles return journey to the house church so when petrol rationing was introduced we stopped going there. We had made many friends, some of whom we still meet at gatherings after 30 years. That church became so big it had to move to new premises.

When Abi was three, she started going to a playgroup for three days a week, from 9.30 a.m. until noon. After the first day she settled in well. It was good for her, an only child, to learn to mix with others and to share toys and games, and to be without her Mum for a while. After the play group Abi attended a pre-school. We noticed, when Abi was about four and had learnt the colours of "Smarties" (sweets with coloured sugar coating), that she suddenly got the colours wrong. We told our osteopath about this, and he asked if she had been delivered by forceps. We told him she had. He said the forceps had dented her skull at the place where sight was affected and he took an X-ray to prove his point. He gave her some cranial massage and her ability to tell colours returned to normal.

When Abi started going to first school at the age of four and a half, she also began to receive glandular treatment. I had to keep a check on her growth and weight as well as on her state of health. Mixing with other children she seemed to pick up various infections one after the other. She had mumps which she passed on to me, though not to her father, also colds, and ear infections.

In September 1975 she started going to the local primary school. While at this school Abi began attending ballet classes and Brownies, and the Sunday school at the Baptist Church. So there was plenty of activity. She did well in the "hostess test" for the Brownies, preparing food for a tea party. She enjoyed the ballet and performed at the Palace Theatre.

On Abi's seventh birthday, a friend and his companion were staying with us while engaged in a crusade in Evesham. One of them gave an entertainment to her party guests. This man gave her his puppet, "Emu", in exchange for a phonographic viewer that he said would help him in his work with children. This viewer was like a television set into which you put stories from the Bible and stories for children. Later in her 7$^{th}$ year of age she had a long illness. She had influenza, tonsillitis, and bronchitis. She seemed to be forever on antibiotics. One day she was passing the lining of her bowel and the doctor told us to get to the hospital fast. He phoned from our house and told me a bed was available and to take her in myself, wrapped up and laid on the back seat. It was only 9 miles to the hospital at Bromsgrove and I knew, before the doctor said so, that she'd be sent there. When I got there, carrying her on my back, I was told it would be "barrier" nursing, and I was to put on special garments, cover my head in a cap and wash carefully, and so on. Abi was very weak and limp in my arms and doctors came to take swabs for tests. They gave instructions she was to drink only water – a small glass every quarter of an hour.

Harold phoned the minister from Redditch Assembly of God Church, and he came out to pray over her straight away. He said it was an attack of the enemy and we must be prepared to say "yes" to whatever God willed, even if it meant her going to be with him. He prayed a deliverance prayer and we offered her back to God. In the morning all tests proved negative but they kept her in for observation for another day.

She was too ill to go back to school for the rest of that term, so she got behind the rest of the class and became discouraged. Instead of being top she dropped down almost to the bottom and this had a very bad impact on her life at school.

Shortly before Abi reached her 8$^{th}$ birthday, her doctor suggested that a child psychologist might be able to find out if there were psychological causes for the eczema, asthma, and other illnesses. She drew a picture of our house that was very advanced for her age and she told him he should not smoke! When he came to see her in her home surroundings she let him sit with her on her rocking horse. This horse had been made for her by a friend and was strong enough for a 14 stone adult to sit on. The result of the psychologist's work with her was that she was a step ahead of us, playing one of us off against the other!

Abi's first experience of caravanning was one Easter when we parked our van at my parents' home, and her granddad taught her to ride her bicycle on the private drive. She participated in a postal

Sunday school that had an assembly nearby for all who were taking part.  Abi enjoyed this.

Sometime later, Harold and I went to a camp at a camp at Ulverston.  After only one night there in the Lake District we had to return home.   Abi had gone to a Brownie camp in Wales, but had developed chickenpox.  Diana, who was then living with our parents, collected Abi from Wales, but we did not want Mother or Dad to get shingles which can be very painful.  In the event, none of us caught it.

At times problems arose at Abi's school.  Around the 31$^{st}$ October, Halloween, they made black cats and witches that were hung on the wall.   Abigail was so fearful that I went to the headmaster and explained what we felt about this practice and how it affected Abigail.   It was not a good spiritual influence for other children either.   Another time Abi locked herself in the bathroom whilst getting dressed for school.  She would not come out without much coaxing and would not go to school.  We found out that this was because she was being bullied.  We sought advice and encouraged her to make friends with the bully and invite her to tea so we could meet her.  We prayed for the girl and her home situation, and for the school to keep an eye on things.   It was at a school sports afternoon that I had evidence that what Abi had told us was true.   God answered our prayer when we found another school for her.

We had intended her to go to a school in Malvern.  However, for various reasons, this was not to be.  We asked God for guidance on the school he had in mind for her.  We knew that it would help her if classes were small as she had missed a lot of schooling through illness.  We heard of the school we finally chose through a colleague at Harold's work place.  Her husband was an inspector of school and he recommended it.  Class size was only eight children.  It was a boarding school but children could go home on four weekends each term from Friday evening to Sunday evening.  This meant we could still go camping together.  We went to see over it and to meet the headmistress before sending Abi there.   We were able to pay for her uniform from an annuity my mother had taken out for her at her birth.  She started at the age of nine.

We supported all the usual school functions – open days, plays, sports and so on. Harold even entered a wheelbarrow race with his dog instead of a barrow and with Abi running alongside to guide him. They were awarded a prize for winning the race, though some people thought they should have been disqualified as the rules were not followed in their case.

As I remembered how I hated my own boarding school I wrote several letters in sealed envelopes for Abi to open if she felt homesick. When she came home at the end of her first term the letters were still unopened, so she must have been happier than I was!

Children in the older forms had exchange visits with families in France. Abi went on one of these, and later we offered to have two French girls but they only stayed for a day and a night and asked to be moved on as they had expected a home with children, not "an old couple"!

**Abi and Jesus**

When Abi was still very young she saw the scar on my tummy and she asked what it was. I explained that I did not make a big enough hole for her to be born the natural way so the doctors had to make a hole there to get her out. The scar was where they had stitched the hole up again. Near her birthday in December she showed signs of distress and I wondered what could have been the cause. She knew that Jesus was born on Christmas day and also that he lives inside us. Her little mind reasoned that Jesus would be born out of her tummy! I was able to put her mind at rest but it taught me that children can worry over what we say to them. She soon afterwards asked if Jesus lived in our loft as the loft opening was just above her bed. I got out the ladder and took her up to see what was there.

When Abi was seven she came into the lounge where we were chatting with friends. She said, "Jesus has told me to give my life to him tonight." So we all joined in prayer with her and felt it was a happy and genuine giving of her life to him. She did not witness to anyone else what she had done, and years later she confessed she did not do it, but wanted to stop our pressure on her to be born again. She confessed because she did not want to be a hypocrite any longer. Being wise after the event I can now see the harm done by my desire for her to be born again, damage that continued to affect her in later life.

On several occasions Abi's school friends came camping with us and occupied the spare bunk. One of these friends, while with us at a Farm camp, gave her life to the Lord. A year or so later, after Abi was baptised at another camp, this friend was baptised there too by full immersion. She had to get permission, so we phoned her parents and they phoned all her Godparents who agreed by phone to the farm. This was an answer to prayer. We had a big tea party and friends from our church came and were also baptised. There were at least nine. The Anglican Church baptises mainly infants but we believe in believers' baptism. A stream, with a dam by a bridge to a sheep dip, sufficed at that farm for many a person to be fully immersed.

## CHAPTER SEVEN: WITNESS
### A car for Stan Woods

While I was still single, I met the Rev. Stan Woods, once the Pastor of a parish near Bridgenorth. He was giving a talk at a house group in Much Wenlock. He spoke about his visit to Guyana to build a church (both worshipers and building). Little did I know then that we would be friends for ever after and involved in joint ministry. I invited him to come to talk to the Guild of Health and to my group at *The Heritage.*

One day God spoke to me saying I was to buy back a car that I had recently sold to a dealer in Kidderminster, and give it away to Stan. It was an Austin 1100 that my Father had given me, and was sold in part exchange for a new car that cost £500. I phoned the bank to see how much I had in my account. The bank had £375, the exact sum the garage had allowed me for it. It was the first time I had ever been asked to give away this amount which was a large sum in those days. I then phoned the garage to ask if I could buy it back, and would confirm next day that I wanted to do so.

I then contacted Stan to say God had told me he needed a car and he could have my old one if he could come to collect it. He was quite amazed, but said he did need a car, and he could come for it in a couple of days. My phone went out of order so I had to go to my parent's house to use theirs to ring the dealer again to confirm I wanted to buy the Austin. The salesman said, "It's a good thing you phoned now, as if you had left it until later the car would have gone to another person who was after it." It needed God's word of knowledge to secure it for Stan. When I told my Father this he said he would pay the £500 for my new car, so I was £125 better off for obeying God's directions. God is no man's debtor. "Give and it shall be given unto you."

Stan did come back a couple of days later to collect it. He travelled by train but missed his connection and so had to take a later train. While I was on the platform at the station waiting for him, the Holy Spirit gave me this information, just before the station announcer came on the Tannoy system saying, "Will a Miss Pheysey, waiting for the Reverend Woods, go to the station office please." I went and was told he would be on the next train after the one I was due to meet.

Having had my home and cars blessed by ministers, I asked Stan to bless my new car. I had a friend in the back and when he performed this task it led to her giving her life to Christ right there in the car.

There is a sequel to the story of Stan's new car. Stan and his wife, Brenda, were just moving to a new area. Stan saw a house up for sale there that he liked, but had little money to put down on it. The house belonged to a lady who went to the Methodist church and who knew that the Woods were coming into the area. He hesitated when a deposit was mentioned, saying they would let her know. The lady, knowing he liked it, then spontaneously offered to lend them the deposit until such time as they could afford to pay it. The house had a garage that Stan thought he might let, not having a car.

This was the very time when I phoned to tell him God said that my old car was to be his!

Stan's eldest brother, George, not a believer at the time, was constantly telling him he was a fool for leaving a well paid job to work in the church. This brother visited Stan and Brenda after their move, and started calling Stan a fool again. Stan replied, "George, you are right. If I were back in my old job I could buy a house". "Yes", George said. Then Stan added, "also a car". "Now you're talking" said his brother. Stan went on, *George, you are sitting in the house and the car is in the garage – so you can see how good God is and how he does provide for our needs."*

Sometime later, after Stan had moved to a new parish, he invited me to have three days with him in April. It was during lent, and also it was the anniversary of my experience of being born again at *Lee Abbey*. He asked me to give my testimony and healing in his church at services and also at morning and evening group meetings.

**Witness to a former teacher**

I was also able to witness in letter writing to those I knew from previous years, one of whom was my old form mistress from school, Bridget Royle. I told her of my conversion in a Christmas letter and as a result of this she felt she could write and tell me of her need for help and prayer for her husband who had been to London to see one of their daughters off on holiday and while he was there a bus had run over his foot. The foot required an operation. When he was under the anaesthetic they found his lungs were not working as they should, so they examined them and found he had cancer and gave him two years to live. He was put onto several prayer lists but he later died. She married again and we are still in touch. She has also been a great blessing in praying for us during Harold's latest illness as she has had similar problems in her life, her second husband having recently died.

The way we live and witness in our homes can also have a far-reaching effect. Having been a member of Kidderminster Photographic Society for some years, I invited the club to come and do some photography in Belbroughton and to have tea with me afterwards. A lady who was the president at the time said, over her cup of tea, "Why do you have a cross over the fire place?" This gave me an opening to explain my faith in Christ and the healing work in which I was involved. She said she did not believe in any of that sort of thing, so I changed the subject after explaining my grandfather had made the cross himself out of a piece of wood from a tree in the garden, yew I think, which is a very hard wood. He had no proper tools but had worked hard to create a cross with a firm round block at its base, all in one. He gave it to me just before he died so it had sentimental value as well. Only one week later her son, who was at college in Manchester, had a terrible accident, falling from his bedroom window to the ground several floors below. It happened in the early hours and he was discovered by a milk van delivering early milk. His injuries were severe and he was not expected to live. His father phoned me saying, "Because of what you said last week I'm asking you and your group if you would pray for my son, Ian." He told me what had happened and of the many bones that were broken – fractured skull, broken arms, ribs and leg. His wife had gone to be with Ian and to help look after him. I went straight to my bedroom and prayed until I had the "all clear" that he would live. Many, many, months later I met Ian. He thanked me for the prayers that had been offered up on his behalf. The only residual problem he was left with was double vision and this was corrected by wearing glasses. He knew he had been saved from death and, knowing he knew this, I said, "Come along to a coffee bar at Chawn Hill, Stourbridge. There you can meet up with other young people who can help you to find out why." He gave his life to Jesus there but I have not had any further news after that.

## Mourners

Another place God can use us is to comfort those who mourn. After a funeral relatives often go back to the grave to look at the flowers and cards. I had gone into the village and saw cars at the church and I went up the steps into the churchyard to see people who were visiting a grave. What an opportunity to give them the Christian hope that death is not the end but that Christ lives on and that he died so that we might have life eternal. One can have ready to hand tracts or little booklets explaining the Christian view of death. A very good one that I had which is now out of print was called, *"For those who mourn"*[20]. All who had a copy told me how much it had helped them.

Everywhere we go we have the chance to bless those God puts beside us, whether on a bus, in a queue, in a shop or at a party. Keep your ears open to the Lord's voice to hear his message for them, or to meet their need.

## Mrs. Bean

Mrs Bean was one such person who came into my life casually this way. She was herself "full of years" but she lived long enough to give me three different size Pyrex basins for a wedding present. They are still in use today. In the short time I visited her at her little home with its cottage garden I had cups of tea with her. She was a blessing to me as much as I was to her. Being a blessing to others can be very exciting, but also very costly in time, energy, petrol, money, and in prayer. Some folks can become very demanding of individual attention and become a drain spiritually, so one has to be in the Lord's will to cope with it all, his grace being sufficient for each day.

## Mrs Shirlaw

On my way to the post box in the village one afternoon I saw a lady sitting on a seat that had been erected around a tree near the post box. I sent an arrow prayer to the Lord, "Is this a job for me to do?" I sat down beside her. She said she was going to tea at a nearby house, but had arrived a little early and had a migraine headache so decided to sit on this seat in the fresh air. Her name was Mrs.

---

[20] For Those Who Mourn", Talbot Press, SPCK, Saffron Waldron, Essex

Shirlaw, and she had just lost her husband. She was having trouble with the will and all the settling up and she would have to move house. I then told her of the Guild of Health, and asked if she would like to come with me to have help and healing. She did come and we were friends for the rest of her life. I once took her to *Lee Abbey* for a holiday. We were still seeing each other after my daughter was born. What if I had not stopped to talk to her that afternoon? She lived 10 years from when I first met her. Nothing happens to me by chance, fate or accident. I believe everything is planned or allowed by God so it is a God incidence, especially when it involves meeting people we don't know. The reason or purpose may take years to unfold.

**Others converted**

Meryl and I had prayed for more persons to be saved and God brought more to join us in the parish after individual befriending, helping and witness, including the witness of outside speakers to whose talks we took people. God used holiday homes, Christian gatherings and the gift of books to reach these persons, six in all. We all began praying for a chance to witness and give testimony in our own church. This came about through a set of circumstances by which God organised an opening for this to happen. In 1967 our minister was taken ill and there was no one else available to lead the Lent Study in Broome church. The minister said that these six persons could each do one of the six Lent "sermons" and that we could run the services between us. We could not have thought of this way of doing it ourselves. It was God's doing.

When it was my turn, I talked on the theme, "What is a Christian?" The Lord's calming, guiding, and gentle influence and his word enabled me to face the Lent congregation of 60 people. (As the church holds only 70 it was nearly full.) I started by reading some scriptures on what makes you a Christian. I went on to speak of salvation and gifts from the Holy Spirit, and what knowing Christ involved and really meant to me. I only had 20 minutes but I managed to cover these points. It was the same for all the other Christians who led one evening each for a period of six weeks. It seemed a success and we had to pray for grace not to get swollen heads or become proud – devices that the enemy can use to destroy the good work done.

Sometimes I used notes and I have kept these. I did not always use them. Sometimes I trusted that the Spirit would fill my mouth when I opened it. God gave me encouragement by Scripture Union notes that I had at the time which said, "Go, for the Lord has sent you. Go, for the people need you. Go, for the word is in you. Just loosen your tongue and talk about Jesus and his word will come through you." Also, the Bible says, "For this purpose I have raised thee up, that I might show my power in thee and that my name might be declared throughout the earth."[21]

Then the 'Old Devil' stepped in again by using born again Christians to say, "You're upsetting people by giving them meat when they can only take milk. Don't say anything that will put their backs up. Put a damper on it or they will think it is all emotionalism. Don't give anything that will offend them or they won't want any more." Jesus said, "Give all, and do not take the easy way out, by not being any different from them. Let your light shine. Do not keep hidden things I have revealed to you. Make my way of life known." The "give all" was said three times so I had confidence to do just that. I committed my spirit entirely to him for him to use as he pleased not fearing what man might say. Christ warns of three things that might happen if we are afraid of people:

We might put on a front; we might hide our faith; we might miss opportunities.

These things happen easily if people's opinions of us are more important to us than God's opinion.

When Jesus entered Jerusalem on Palm Sunday, there were those who tried to silence his followers. He said that if the disciples held their peace, then the very stones would cry out. It is also written, "Cast not away your confidence which hath great recompense and reward. Hold fast to the faith without wavering... If any man draws back God has no pleasure in him. We are not of them that draw back unto perdition but of them that believe in the saving of the soul"[22]. To suppress Good News and keep silent is to incur guilt. We should

---

[21] Romans 9 17
[22] Hebrews 10: 35-39

witness with all boldness. These sayings all showed that I should carry on as I had been doing.

There were 11 talks during this period. Examples of the titles were: "What has God done?" "Receiving Christ", "The Abundant Life", "Healing and Wholeness in Christ", "Salvation", "Sonship", "Faith and Works."

During this period, eighteen sick people were visited, prayed with, and ministered to. Some were later sent booklets and letters. I did all the arranging and booking of venues and speakers for two weekend conferences on Healing. I taped the talks and sent them out later for those unable to attend.

**Witness at Ridley Hall, Cambridge 1969**

An invitation came from our friend, Mike Hall, to go to speak in the lunch hour about "The Ministry of Healing at Ridley Hall, Cambridge, where he was now in training for the Ministry. When I put this invitation to God in prayer the answer came by the sung words, "Go tell it on the mountains, over the hills and far away"[23]. I felt that was clear enough to accept the invitation, but who was I to go to tell such men about the healing ministry.

When the actual date was given me it clashed with an appointment that Harold had to see a skin specialist about a rash on his leg. Also we needed to know if the Guide Dogs for the Blind Association would have Kim for the weekend. The dermatologist changed the appointment without our asking, and Kim could go to Leamington for 3 days. We thought this was more confirmation. (We say a decision must be right in the heart, the word, and the circumstances.)

My notes for this talk on The Ministry of Healing came easily. I mentioned the different words used to describe the healing ministry and the different methods used. I told my audience of places where they could learn more and what the study of the Bible could teach them on the subject. I explained the qualities that are needed in the would-be healer and how important it is to follow through and to have back up. I warned them of common mistakes and stressed that God must always be given the glory.

After the talk we all went back to Mike's residence. Then Harold and I went into town. Harold said, "We ought to take something in the food line as a present since they are feeding us and others." We

---

[23] Junior Praise hymnbook

89

stood by the pork pie counter in a supermarket and he said, "Get one of those". I saw some large frozen ducks so we bought one of those too.

When we returned and handed over our gifts we were amazed to learn that Mike had said in his prayer time that morning that if someone gave him a pork pie that day he would know for sure God's will over a certain matter! The duck also helped to feed the group.

After the meal one of Mike's sons, aged only about six, prayed for Harold's sight and Harold then saw the buttons on Mike's jacket. They were leather with a cross on them. We all rejoiced and then it was time to go home.

## Witnessing in Bath

It was in July 1970 that we had been invited to give a talk to people in Bath. We had a short rest before the evening meeting. Then, after my talk, another group met at the farmhouse. Further help and healing and advice were given to members of the family who came for refreshments. There was so much need that we did not realise how the hours were passing. Some of the children were studying false and occult religions for their Religious Education lessons and they had got into trouble with evil spirits through this searching. We led them to see their need of Jesus as their Lord and Saviour. This was out on the lawn at 2.00. a.m.!

## Lay Witness Mission 1977

When we were chatting with other campers at Spitten Farm they asked us if we knew of the Lay Witness Mission. This organisation could do with people with testimonies like ours. It began when a Christian who lived in England was told to go to Spokane in America to see the Lay Witness Mission there. Born again believers were willing to go, at their own expense, to give help and witness at weekend missions in various churches to lead people to Christ the Lord. They gathered to pray for renewal before each weekend event. On the Friday night there was a dinner, open to the entire parish, when several of the missioners gave ten-minute testimonies. On the Saturday there was a coffee morning and Bible study groups, and on Sunday the missioners gave their testimony in the church at morning service. The church which held the mission offered accommodation to the missioners. The Englishman came back so fired-up that he wanted to start the same thing in England which he did.

We were told that if we were interested in becoming missioners we could contact the head of the Lay Witness Mission about training. We felt led to join and went to Bolsover for the instruction weekend. We were shown how to give testimony, run a coffee morning, lead a Bible study, and run a service. We also learned how to listen, how to give counselling and how to help enquirers. We were passed as suitable ambassadors for Christ, and were declared to be "Soul Winners" on August 10th that year at Spitten Farm.

We were called upon to go for our first mission to Holmsfield. Before we went, a letter came introducing us to the people with whom we would be staying, a lovely lady who had been a nurse and her husband. They had been unable to have children of their own because of illness, but there were many children in the family of God whom they had led to the Lord. When the day for the start of the mission arrived we were welcomed with open arms. Nothing was too much trouble. They had even vacated their double bed to allow us to sleep together. They welcomed Honey, the guide dog, as well.

We had some refreshments before going to the church to meet our leader and other missioners. There the vicar put us in the picture regarding the type of people we would meet, the way we would be placed at the meal, and who would be called upon to testify. To conclude this preliminary gathering we prayed together for the whole weekend.

The Friday evening dinner meeting turned out to be wonderful. There was lots of interest, and people mixed in very well with one another. Afterwards we stayed up late chatting with our host and hostess before going to bed for a restful night's sleep.

The Saturday coffee morning was held so we could mix with the parishioners again, some of them being different from the night before. This brought out many of the people's needs and their opinions and faith and what they thought about evangelism. In the afternoon everyone was invited to have tea with a lady who had a lovely old mansion. (We had met her before as she had a sister who lived in Worcester whom she visited. She decided to come over to see us before the start of the mission.) I remember her tea well, because I was handing Harold a cup from behind the sofa where he was sitting. He put his hand up at the same time and bumped mine, so the cup toppled, and spilt tea over his trousers. He stood by the fire to dry them off. I had not taken spare trousers so he put his pyjamas on under the damp ones for the Saturday evening meeting.

This began with the prayer group and the leader had decided we should both give our testimony then. All went well and people came up to speak with us afterwards and to ask further questions.

On Sunday we had all been allotted our tasks in the service, which was well attended.

After lunch we set off for home and to collect our daughter Abigail from the cousin, Christine, who had looked after her. We learnt she had played with our cousin's own three children. Christine had attended to all Abigail's medical needs.

We kept in touch with our Holmsfield hostess for several years afterwards until she died. We were booked to do a similar Lay Witness Mission at Boston, but had to cancel because our daughter was taken to hospital seriously ill. In the end we never went on another of their missions as we felt it was our duty to put Abigail first.

We kept in touch with what was going on, but for some reason these missions ceased and were replaced by other forms of evangelism, Billy Graham's crusades for instance. Also we were invited to join another Evangelical group called the Full Gospel Business Men's Fellowship International.

**The Full Gospel Business Men's Fellowship International**

This organisation was started in America by Demos Shakarian. He had a vision which God used to inspire him to form this fellowship. He wrote a book about it called *"The Happiest People on Earth"*[24]. The FGBMFI is not a church or a sect. It has no priests or pastors and does not start churches. Its aims are:

> To call men to God and into the church by witnessing to
> God's presence and power in the world today through the
> message of the total Gospel for the total man.
> To provide a basis for Christian fellowship among men
> everywhere under the single banner of their experience in

---

[24] "The Happiest People on Earth", Demos Shakarian, Elizabeth Sherrill and John Sherrill, Hodder 1979

Jesus Christ, and to strengthen them so they can go back to their churches refreshed and renewed.

To bring about a greater measure of unity among all Christians.

We went to their chapter at Worcester to see what they were really like. We joined and for many years we went to their dinner meetings and days of fasting and prayer for the nation. There were also workshops and rallies and weekend retreats.

We took friends, both saved and unsaved, with us to FGBMFI dinners. It was interesting to see their reactions, especially the reactions of our minister whom we took to one of the dinners.

We found, in the end, that few unsaved visitors attended and the reason why Christians went was because they had nothing like it in their own churches or villages and they were hungry for more of God and Jesus and the Holy Spirit.

Dr. Calcott, the friend whom we had contacted to see if he could help our daughter's eczema, himself became president of the Full Gospel Business Men's Fellowship International at Worcester.

The FGBMFI publishes a magazine called "Voice" in which we read many wonderful testimonies, including miracles of healing. We bought extra copies so we could give them away to anyone who came to our home, whether known to us, or strangers. We also left copies in waiting rooms, buses and other places where they could be read. "Voice" also became an instrument of passing on the good news. This practice we have continued right up to the present time.

We stayed with the Worcester branch until it closed down after some years. As people died or moved away, the attendance declined. When this happened it was decided to close down, but, as I write, some are thinking of restarting it.

The FGBMFI has gone from America all around the world and their "Voice" is now printed in 26 different languages.[25]

**Witness to the Business and Professional Women's Association**

Abigail happened to mention to the Secretary at her school in 1981 that I gave talks about healing. The Secretary was a member of the

---

[25] The UK field Office address of FGBMFI is PO BOX 11, Knutsford, Cheshire, WA16 6QP. Telephone 01565 632667

Business and Professional Women's Association which was looking for speakers. She asked if I would be a speaker at one of their meetings. I agreed, and, after getting prayer support, I went along and gave my testimony. When I told them that I had failed the secondary school entrance examination ("Eleven Plus") and had never sat for any later examinations, they were amazed that I had the confidence to speak as I did about my faith. I told them that they could have the same faith if they took the same steps that I had taken. A lady in the audience said she was a member of a meditation group, and through this person I was invited to speak to that group.

**Witness to a Transcendental Meditation Group**

When invited by telephone to speak to this group, I asked what kind of group it was. The caller replied, "Christian Meditation". I was a little suspicious and got prayer support to cover me for the evening. The lady in whose house they met asked me into a separate room to discuss the order of the meeting. She would do the prayers, then she would introduce me, and refreshments would be provided after my talk. I asked if I could visit the bathroom first. Whilst I was there, the Lord said to me, "You are on enemy territory here". I said, "I'm not afraid of him. I will go ahead and give my talk." At the start of the meeting, the lady said, "Tonight Mrs. Bagby will do the prayers as well as give her talk, and then we will have some tea." So I began by placing the whole evening in God's hands and asking the Holy Spirit to guide our thoughts and what I said." I gave my talk and asked if there were any questions. One lady said she was a Christian Spiritualist. I said, "You cannot possibly be both, it is either one or the other." I then told her how I had been involved in spiritualism for seven years before I realised that it was not the truth or the way and gave my life to Jesus instead. One man said, "If what you say is true, you frighten me." I told him that what I said was the truth and was a wake-up call to him to consider his ways. Another man sat at the front, and when I said I believed the Bible was inspired by the Holy Spirit and true, and I hoped they believed the same, there was a deadly hush. No one spoke to support me. After the refreshments I went home and phoned my prayer supporters to tell them what had happened.

**Witness to my own mother**

At a healing service in 1969 in Henley in Arden both Harold and I sought help and healing and to learn more about the healing ministry. The speaker said that repentance is often followed by a miracle. At this service I said to God, "I will not try again to get Mum to give her life to you. I will leave it entirely to your Spirit to convict and convert her. I will expect you to save her before Christmas."

This was harder than I had expected because the next day I went over to *The Park* (where Mother lived) and was telling her about the previous day's healing service. I suddenly realised that what I was doing was breaking my promise to God so soon after making it. Mother went upstairs to rest on her bed after lunch. I then went into the drawing room and broke into tears of repentance, thinking I would have done untold harm and would have set back the chance of Mum being saved. Mum saw later that I had been crying, so she asked why. I explained to her my promise, and how I had broken it. I had cried before God for wrong doing and had promised not to preach at her again, or try to win her for the Lord, but would leave it to him. I said that I had expected it to happen by Christmas, but I had put my foot into it, because I so desperately wanted her to be saved before she died. I wanted our family to be complete in heaven, all praising God together. Mum said, "I do believe so and so, this, that, and the other." I replied, "Mum, you've done the believing and the good works (doing) but you haven't repented and received Jesus as your own Saviour and Lord." She then said, "You say a prayer and I will say it with you." That's how she gave her life to Jesus, aged 76 and the Lord used me when I had least expected him to. When we let go and let God, miracles do happen and he can work more rapidly.

## CHAPTER EIGHT: GUIDE DOGS
### Kim

Harold's first dog was Candy Floss, but that was before I met Harold, so Candy was not part of my life as Kim was. As mentioned in connection with my courtship, the National Dog Owners' Association had awarded Kim their medal for taking herself to the vet, thus saving her own life. She was an amazing dog in other ways. One day, as we were travelling, she suddenly shot up from between Harold's feet on the floor and put her head up through the steering wheel. Harold slapped her down because she could have caused an accident. After this she became more and more reluctant to get into the car. The Guide Dogs for the Blind Association were told and they advised us to dope her if necessary. Well, the car was due to be serviced, but its guarantee had just expired when we took it in. The garage found a cracked gear box. The dog knew it was unsafe and tried to show us. It must have happened on the trip when she jumped up. The garage therefore took that as the time when it happened which was still in the guarantee period, so we did not have to pay for it, thanks to Kim.

One day, Kim had been at the church with Harold at a communion service. She was taking him up the aisle to the altar when she collapsed and fell over and looked spark out. She recovered and got home. The vet, who had been phoned, arrived at the same time. He diagnosed that her heart had not received the message from her brain that tells it to beat. This caused her to black out and it could happen at any time in the future. It might put the dog and Harold in a dangerous situation.

When our daughter, Abi was small, my Mother felt that it was not a good plan to have a sick dog in the house. Kim had a heart problem, an eye problem, and displacement of the hip. She was 14 years old, so she had done a full span of service.

Mother came to stay with us while Father was in London on business. She said she would like to have a chat about Kim. She said, "Don't you think it's time Harold changed Kim for another dog?" Harold came back to ask what we wanted for our night cap, tea, coffee, or cocoa. I said, "Listen to what Mater has just said to me about Kim." Mother then said to Harold, "Now you are a father I think you should realise your responsibilities to your wife and daughter. Don't you think it's time to have Kim put to sleep and to get another dog as she is unhealthy and she could be the cause of Abigail's skin trouble?"

This was a total shock to Harold. Instead of getting our night cap drinks he went to the bathroom to get ready for bed. He went to the Lord in prayer and as he knelt down he felt the sheepskin rug and thought of Gideon and his fleece. He said to God, "If this is you speaking to me, I want £500 on my breakfast plate in the morning. "

He thought this would be impossible as the post did not come before he left for work. He said nothing to Mum or to me about this prayer. He got up at 5.45 a.m., showered, dressed, had his quiet time, groomed the dog and came to breakfast. He had just sat down when Mother came in and sat beside him. (She had never done this before.) She said, "You know, Harold, if you decide to do what I said last night, I would be prepared to pay the price of a new one." Harold asked her if she knew the price of a dog and what it costs to train one. She replied, "I have heard that they cost about £250, but it would not matter if it were twice that amount." Here was the £500 on his breakfast table, so Harold knew what he had to do. When he was at work he phoned the Guide Dogs for the Blind Association to ask them to come and fail Kim, but when he got through he was too choked up to speak so he pulled the plug out. At the third try he managed to get the request out to the person at the other end. They came and failed Kim and put in motion the form requesting another dog. You don't have to pay more than 50p for a dog, but Harold had already had Candy Floss and Kim for 50p and felt he would like to give the full price for the third one.

It's a six-week wait, which seemed a very long time when you know it will be "Goodbye" to one and "Hello" to another. Harold thought Kim deserved a happy retirement and prayed to the Lord for that to happen. Knowing I would need support to get to the GDBA Centre at Leamington with Harold and Kim, God sent a lady to help me. We had only gone a couple of miles when Harold felt he could not go through with it. He pulled the hand brake and I felt the car swerve and come to a halt. I wondered what on earth was wrong until he owned up to what he had done.

We decided to pray there and then in the car and ask the Lord to show us his solution. We started off again in a far better frame of mind. The GDBA had requested that Kim be put down because she was so well known for the feat of saving her own life before. They were therefore very surprised to see Harold turn up at Leamington with her. Harold would be there for a month and they said they would let Kim stay in their kennels for a fortnight.

When we arrived at the Centre, Kim was taken to the kennels and Harold was taken to the head man who said he would feel differently when he had the new dog. They would get him to sign the papers then.

When I went to see him at the weekend I bumped into a kennel maid taking Kim for a walk. Kim recognised me, and I rushed to Harold nearly in tears myself.

Mother invited me to stay at her home for the month that Harold would be away. She could look after Abi when I went to see him. We were having alterations done to the gas water heater so there would not be hot water available at our home, *Fair Haven,* for nappies.

The first fortnight went by. Harold was in the lounge and sensed that it was Mr. Moody, the head man, who came to sit beside him. Harold said, "It's no good you bringing me those papers to sign because I won't do it." Mr. Moody then explained that he would not have to, because the kennel maid had asked permission to take Kim to her home. Her father was head gardener at Hampton Court so Kim would have lots of room there. (In fact she had already been there and had pulled out all the border plants that he had just been put in!)

The Kennel maid's request was the answer to the prayer we had made in the car on our way to Leamington and Harold was delighted. We were given news of her for the rest of her life and she is buried somewhere in the grounds of Hampton Court. (Years later we went there to a flower show but did not find any tombstone for a dog)

We think Kim's successful placement led to the GDBA considering retiring dogs to homes, or remaining with owners along with their new dog, instead of putting them down.

Mother had said to Harold that she would rather that he did not have an Alsatian as there had been stories in the newspapers of Alsatians savaging children. In the nineteen-seventies, Alsatians formed a much larger percentage of the breeds trained than they do today. Training dogs to be the "Seeing Eye" for the blind (the term used in the U.S.A.) began with Alsatians. It is said that a Mrs. Eustace, who lived in Switzerland, had noticed how brainy Alsatians were, since she had several herself. She hired a Russian dog trainer, Captain Liakov, to teach them to do tricks. This was reported in the "*Readers' Digest*" and an American had the story read to him. He said, "If your dogs are so clever, why not train them to lead the blind?" Then people who were in the "*Tail Wagers Club*" offered some of their Alsatian puppies for the job. Only a few were trained to start with but later the GDBA bred and trained its own dogs and had fewer failures as a result.

## Mitzie

Mitzie, Harold's new dog, was the biggest black and tan Alsatian. She was perfect with children, a real charmer. She was so big that she took up nearly all the back seat of the car. Abi's baby seat was in the corner next to Mitzie which was even worse for the eczema from which she suffered. (It was only later we got an estate car to accommodate the dog.)

When we got home from Leamington I realised that I had forgotten to buy any dog food, so Harold went up to the butcher's with Mitzie while I unpacked and put the car in the garage. When Harold started for home again he suddenly wondered if the dog would be able to find the way. Even if he gave her directions to the street she would still have to find the house. She came straight to it, even though there was no car outside for her to smell her own scent. To give her more exercise we used to let her out of the car at the top of the street. She would run down the pavement and jump over the fence into our entry. Then she was fed and we would let her in by the back door.

Normally, when we had a new dog, we would say, for example, "Go to the butcher's" and I would go to this shop and back with Harold who had the dog on a leash, not in harness. An hour later he would harness her up and say, "Go to the butcher's", or to the church, the dentist, the grocer's or wherever. The procedure was the same. They went on the leash with me and afterwards on their own.

Today it is very different. The trainer comes and brings the dog. The dog then has a weekend to get used to the home and to us. Then the trainer comes five days a week for a month. The dogs learn short distances, then longer ones. When they have learnt the routes they are given a test. The dog and owner are watched by the trainer and another GDBA person. These two people then decide if the dog is ready to be passed as fit to go out on their own. Harold just says the destination and does not have to say all the "lefts" and "rights" and other commands that he must use with a new dog. Weekly and monthly reports are given for six months.

Harold was asked if he would be willing to be a guide dog owner speaker for our area. He said he would. They had speakers' training days at the Centre at Leamington which we attended. This led to more invitations to schools, Women's Institutes, handicapped groups, Boy Scouts, the Round Table, Towns Women's Guilds, Motorists' Association, Over Sixties, Darby and Joan clubs, the British Alsatian Club and others in private houses.

One day Mitzie was in a country lane on the far side of the road from us. We could not let her out in open country because of swine fever. I said to Harold, "There's a car coming." He whistled Mitzie and she obeyed but was hit by the on-coming car. It was not the driver's fault. He stopped and thankfully the dog was only bruised on her shoulder so all was well.

We kept her until she was eight years old. She had to be put to sleep in November 1978 because she had spondylitis and was unable to use her back legs so could not get up steps or jump into the car.

**Perkins**

Mitze was replaced by Honey, then by Nicholas, then by Perkins, a golden Labrador, whom we had for several years. When it was time for him to retire, a visitor from the Guide Dogs for the Blind Association came to see us while we were camping at a place called "Top Barn". The good news was that they had found someone, named Mrs Frost, who wanted to take Perkins for the rest of his life. She was the lady who had originally puppy-walked him. We were delighted because we knew how much Perkins loved her from the excitement he showed when we met her at GDBA open days at Leamington Spa. We had kept in touch with her at Christmas.

We had intended to go to a CCCF Camp at Evesham but never went because GDBA phoned to say they were to start Harold's training with his new dog, Uska, from home on 16<sup>th</sup> September and they wanted us to arrange for Mrs Frost to take Perkins away before that date.

## CHAPTER NINE: FURTHER DEVELOPMENT IN CHRISTIAN LIVING
### Combat with the occult

During one autumn Mrs. Cameron, the lady who had introduced me to my future husband, Harold, invited me to go to a meeting of the Churches' Fellowship for Psychical Studies held at the Deanery in Worcester. I knew nothing about them but was told it was a group that held meetings on different aspects of healing, so I went along. As soon as the meeting started I sensed this was wrong. It was not in the will and way of the Lord for me, since it was like spiritualism. I thanked them, but said I would not like to go to any more. Dangerous dabbling in that realm could have got me into trouble, such as I had had before my conversion. The matter was to come up later in two instances in my life, one with my Mother and another with a lady in a church I attended, so I was glad I had this knowledge. To be forewarned is to be forearmed.

One of the first things I had noticed after my born again experience at *Lee Abbey* was I could not bear to look at anything of the occult. It smelt foul. I got out all the papers, magazines, books and tapes and destroyed them (though one was to appear later in a book case). I wrote to my Aunt Norah and her medium friends that I no longer wanted to have anything to do with Spirits and I never again attended séances, or their services, or their churches. I had found out that all of this was of the Devil (because God raised the blind in my mind to let in light. I could not now witness for the untruth when the One who is the Truth dwelt inside me). They all said, "You go your way and we will still go ours." It was difficult to do when they had been close and good to me. I then started trying to convert them to the truth and they ceased contact, though my Aunt kept in touch.

When Mrs. Cameron's husband was taken very ill with lung cancer, and when he died she asked me if I could put her in touch with the mediums I had known in my past as she wanted to contact him, she was so upset at his death. I refused, saying that I had learnt this was not the right way to go and I did not want to be responsible for sending her to a medium, knowing it is contrary to the truth. She said, "It will be all right. I'm a Christian. I will be protected". She obtained an address from someone else and went to a séance. I've never seen such a rapid change in the looks of a Christian. Her light went out. She died alone in a car park at a conference centre she had attended. It had snowed and no one saw her inside her car until her sister phoned to say she had not returned home. Police went to look for her and found her. I think it was a heart attack.

**Finding Occult Things**

One December, early in our marriage, my husband, Harold, and I both went down with flu. I was the first to have it, so Harold said to his guide dog, Kim, "Come on, we will go to post some letters and then go to the chemist to get your missus something to help her flu." The weather was cold with wet sleet and ice. After posting the letters Harold thought he would go straight home to get warm again. However, Kim had remembered what he had said and she took him to the chemist. He only realised what she had done when she went up the step to the door.

Later that evening I was fighting for breath and felt very ill. Harold went to the bathroom and while there he heard a knock on the front door and went to see who it was. He realised it was Jesus who was standing there so he bade him come in. He did and he healed me, but he also brought to Harold's attention there was something of the enemy in the hall in a book case. Harold said, "Jo, you have to get out of bed and come and see what I am pointing to." There, in the bookcase, was a spiritualist book my Aunt Norah had given me that I had missed when I cleared out all the things I had which were connected with the occult. That had been the means whereby there was an open door for the enemy to come in and attack me as I fought for my breath a few moments before. Harold took the book, tore up the pages, put them in the dust bin and poured water over them to really destroy them.

A short while later my Aunt asked us to return the book, so we told her what had happened to it. In the base of the bookcase, hidden from view, there was also a tape of a séance. That was wiped clean. There was a very clear change in the atmosphere when this had been done. I had been given the hymn, "All ye who seek for sure relief in trouble or distress, whatever sorrow vex the mind or guilt the soul oppress."[26]

---

[26] Latin, 18th century, tr. Edward Caswall (1814-78)

Just before Christ came in to help, Kim was sleeping in a dog bed in the hall. She saw something that made her eyes follow Jesus and her hair stand up along her back.

After this, presents began to arrive for Christmas. As my custom was, I put them all away to be opened on Christmas day. However, I found I was losing my joy and unable to pray and read the Bible as usual. I wondered what was wrong. When we went to the Assembly of God Church for the Christmas Day service, the Pastor came to me and asked what I had been up to. I replied, "Nothing that I know of, Pastor, why?" He said, "You have spirits of the occult around you, so you must have allowed them a doorway." The "doorway" came to light after lunch when we opened our presents. My Aunt Norah had sent me a birthday book with horoscope readings for each day of the year. We phoned Pastor to say we had found the culprit. It's good to have a prayer of deliverance, which he prayed over me in Church, but the discovery of the book confirmed his insight. We enjoyed the rest of Christmas Day and my prayer and Bible reading went back to normal and joy returned to my spirit.

## A Haunted Room at *Lea Abbey*

When I am asked to speak anywhere I ask for a letter of confirmation, or a phone call to remind me a week beforehand, especially if there is some distance between the booking and speaking dates.

In April of 1969 an *Over Sixties Club* had asked me to show them my slides of the Holy Land. The lady who should have reminded me about this was in hospital, but one day her husband, Mr. Lester, stood on my doorstep, having come in person to do the reminding. I invited him in for coffee and we got talking. I mentioned *Lee Abbey* (where I was born again). The following September I was going to take my husband, Harold, there so he could see what a lovely place it was. Mr. Lester said it did not hold happy memories for him. He and his first wife had had a room that looked onto a courtyard with no view of the sea or the countryside. This was a disappointment. What was worse was that his sons had got into difficulties swimming in the bay. They were rescued, but his wife had drowned while trying to save them.

When Harold and I went to *Lee Abbey* we discovered on arrival that I had left Harold's suitcase behind under our bed, where he would not fall over it. So we went to buy him some shirts, pyjamas and underwear as this was cheaper than driving home. When we entered the room we had been given Harold said, "I don't like this room. It feels cold and spooky. What's the view?" I said it looked into an inner courtyard. He did not think much of the evening meal either, and asked why I had booked to come again. That night we put the two single beds together to make one bed. We had not been in it long before we recognised spirits knocking and occult things from our past life. We took the Bible and claimed verses for our protection. Harold said, "Pray for me, I feel as if I am drowning. Do something quickly". I laid my hands upon him, put on "the whole armour of God", claimed the "covering of the Blood"[27] and said, "In the name of Jesus". Harold then said he could hear a tractor and an ambulance in the distance and asked if I could hear it as well. We decided to report it in the morning to the community and went to sleep.

Next morning I went to ask if anything had happened in that room in the past to cause the trouble we had had to deal with. We were told that twenty years earlier a woman had drowned trying to save her sons in the bay. A tractor and trailer had been sent from the farm to bring her body back to that room. I remembered what Mr. Lester had told me and we were sure it was the same room of which he had spoken when he had called on me in March. We had the room prayed over and there was no more trouble thereafter. God had used us for that purpose. So peace reigned.

**Dangers of the Occult**

People do not realise the dangers of dabbling in occult things. Parents living near us asked for help when their daughter had been using an Ouija board in their home. She and school friends had been asking it questions. The family were troubled by all sorts of strange happenings both at home and in the café where they worked. They had nightmare visions of ghostly apparitions and fat spat out and burnt them at the stove. I told them I knew of a minister who could

---

[27] The armour is given in Eph. 6: 10-17; for the protection of the blood see Rev. 5:9

do an exorcism and pray with them both. This he did. He got them to confess they had been involved in the occult and to repent and then he anointed them with oil. There was no more trouble in their home or in the café. It is important to have confession and repentance after involvement in the occult.

We had another nasty occult experience. Harold's Uncle and Aunt stayed for tea one day. His Aunt had a bad leg so, after tea, I offered to pray for it to be healed in Jesus' name. That night, after they had left, I could not feel my legs. It was just as if I had no legs myself. I woke Harold and asked him to pray for me. We both knew it was the Old Devil having a go at me. When no sensation returned we phoned the leader of the house group, in Worcester, of which we were members at the time. It was 1.30 a.m. but the leader, Derek, said God had told him the phone would ring during the night and he was to answer it. Derek prayed a prayer of deliverance over the phone and told Harold to make me a cup of tea and run a bath full of water. I was to get in and have full body cleansing like full immersion baptism. While in the bath I was to pray for complete cleansing, renewal and refreshment. When this had been done he said the problem would probably be solved, but I was to phone him again if there was any more trouble. All was fine and we went back to sleep. I realised how you can be attacked if you fail to plead the blood and to put on the whole armour of God. I had failed to do this because Harold's relatives were both born again believers so I thought there was no need to be careful over those who already have Christ dwelling in them.

The Worcester house group leader, Derek, was involved on another occasion when he called at our house on his way to give a talk to a Baptist group. When he entered our lounge he saw paintings, illuminated pictures, and crosses that he said we must throw out. We should also get rid of some dolls that belonged to our daughter Abi. These things were having an evil influence on us, as were chairs that had come from the home of my Aunt Norah. Mediums had probably sat on these. Derek discerned in the Spirit that the enemy was using these to cause us trouble. We were obedient to his instructions and our health and tempers improved afterwards.

In 1975 we went to a session with another minister on "Healing of the Memories", since he believed that the eczema from which our daughter, Abigail, suffered was partly caused by an unclean spirit from the past. Each year of her life was prayed over. The whole family, even the dog, was put under the Blood of Jesus, so that demonic spirits could find no place to enter and set up home.

**Christian Visitors**

Christian visitors from all over the world, including our own country, gave us much help in our Christian growth. Prior to my being born again, I am sure many of the experiences with visitors would not have taken place. Until then I had only known the clergy of my own and neighbouring parishes. Now, our guests came to us in many ways: by personal recommendation and invitation; through various organisations, groups or fellowships; through conferences, holidays, pilgrimages or crusades; or as a result of lectures or house groups. Learning more about the work of God in other countries had a marked effect on our outlook and life. Countries represented by our visitors included Guyana, Tanzania, Kenya, India, Australia, Canada, Sweden and Germany.

Some visitors came from very hot countries, so we had to keep their rooms warm and give them extra clothes. Some were housed temporarily nearby and needed furniture and bedding. We provided pillows for a choir from Africa. Members of the family of God always enjoy each other's company and the sharing of experiences and of knowledge of Jesus. All wrote in our "Visitors' Book", and all the entries are worth reading. We keep in touch with some of these people, but others have died or dropped away over a thirty year period.

When we had problems, sickness, or worries, a visitor would be sent at the moment of our need.

St Paul instructs us to "Share with God's people who are in need", and to "Practise hospitality."[28] This text showed me that the visits were in God's plan. Some Visitors had written books that I later bought; others had magazines to offer; others sent us prayer sheets and news sheets with updates of their work abroad, so that we could give them prayer support in their ministries. All this enlarged our

---

[28] *Romans 12: 13*

vision of what is going on in the media programmes, church functions, evangelism and healing around the globe.

Meeting people who came from the Third World's poor countries, and who had nothing, made us appreciate all we have in this country. We not only have material possessions, but also freedom of speech, though I hear of restrictions now. Some of the twelve ministers who have stayed here have become well-known through Christian programmes on television. When we had just had cable TV, I got up at 4.00 a.m. to listen to and watch Christian programmes until 7.00 a.m. Cable TV later gave up Christian programmes, and for some years we did not have the channel on our set. However, in 2006 we decided to go digital, and that enabled us to have the God TV Europe channel, through which I have been greatly blessed. I also videoed some programmes for others to see who do not have the channel on their sets.

I have many tapes and videos ordered from Christian sources such as: Westminster School of Theology, Waverley Abbey House, the Crusade for World Revival, Christ for All Nations, the Good News Crusade, Don Summer's Evangelistic Campaign, and, more recently, Joyce Meyer's tapes. These have had impact and brought blessing, and some have been passed on.

**Testing, Trials and Tribulations in Church Life**

We have not seen eye-to-eye with all the vicars at our church. We learnt that we had to love, and not cause rifts, although these sometimes did happen. We also learnt not to undermine those whom God had set in authority over us. We should not retaliate, but keep silent and let God do things in his way. "Vengeance is mine, I will repay, says the Lord".[29] Some of the differences were resolved by the persons involved moving on. Sometimes we moved on. Sometimes things were settled amicably.

We are told by Jesus Christ to expect persecution and trials and misunderstandings and upsets because we are in the world though not of it. We must take up our cross daily if we want to follow Him. One day Diana, my sister, was taken ill and could not teach her Bishop's Certificate Class in Redditch. She phoned to ask if I would

---

[29] Romans 12:19

go to her to collect the material for the class and take it to a minister who was on the course and ask him to take over that evening. I did as she asked but the minister said it was his day off and he would be in Oxford. I went home and wondered why I had been left holding the baby. I went to God in prayer and the answer was that he wanted people with heart experience rather than head knowledge. I went along and told the group I had only gone to deliver the subject matter. I was not the tutor but I did have some knowledge of the subject-matter which was "True and False Prophets". I sat down and someone came across and asked me what I knew of the subject. I replied from my own life's experience, not from a Bible study. Then another came, and in the end all those who were really interested were listening to me. Then someone said, "Your sister never divided the people like you have done", whereupon the rest of the class got up and walked out. In the end we were still talking when the caretaker came to lock up the room. So we went downstairs and outside and continued underneath an archway. Some were so much in need themselves that I took their names and addresses and visited them privately. I even got my Pentecostal Minister to go to one lady who was the daughter of a medium and needed more help than I could give.

Two days later I went on my weekly visit to my parents, and my sister, who was then living above them, heard me arrive and called down to ask if I would go up and see her immediately please. She wanted to know what had happened on the previous Monday class night. Apparently one member of the class was so upset that he or she contacted the Head of Religious Education for the Diocese, and told him that an unauthorised person had gone to take their class. My sister was not to blame in any way, and neither was I really, but it upset me very much to think that my obeying God had caused such uproar and got my sister into trouble. I know that, following this, our minister who had not given me advice about it, was very annoyed. Perhaps he had been spoken to about it. He took it out on me by preaching at me from the pulpit in his sermon. The congregation were not aware of it and we kept silent.

Within two months this minister moved on to another parish. People were not rude or unkind – they just avoided us. They chose not to sit near us unless there was no other seat available. We felt ostracised and misunderstood. We had been going there for 18 years without seeing any change, so we decided it was time for us to go.

We were seeking God's will for the future and went to our friend, Dr. Calcott, for "Praise, Promise, and Problem". He heard from the Lord that we would be shown where to break bread. He even said we could stay with him but he felt we should return home where friends were gathered and holding a prayer meeting. Our daughter rushed out to greet us saying, "You will never guess what's happened!" A piece of bread had fallen down the chimney, and then another. A bird could not have dropped them as the chimney was covered.

We phoned Dr. Calcott who said he saw an angel drop it down. This, we agreed, meant we should hold a house-church at our own home. We did so for 7 years. Some members stayed with us all that time and others came and left. Sometimes couples who were out of work stayed to have lunch with us. We learnt a lot about one another: what faith we had, how we prayed, and so on. It became predictable who would speak and what they would say. The house-church became dull and lifeless. It was a lifesaver to me because it was running at a time when I had thyroid trouble and was very ill.

# CHAPTER TEN: CARS AND CARAVANS AND CAMPS
## Protection while driving

As I do a lot of driving, I always ask the pilot, Jesus, to pilot me wherever I go. I have had some experiences of God's protection. Soon after seat belts were invented, but not yet compulsory, I put mine on. The Lord pointed out that it was not adjusted correctly, not tight enough. This I corrected and I drove more carefully as a consequence. I turned left into a back street in Kidderminster and a child suddenly came running across straight in front of me to a house on the other side of the street. She came out of a street on my left so I had no warning at all. I missed her by inches. A woman walking on the pavement coming towards me saw it all and said, "My word, what a silly child! Are you all right?" She suggested that I should go after the child and tell her off, but I did not stop to do that. A few minutes later, at the butcher's shop, the assistant asked if I was all right as I looked very pale. I told him I had had the fright of my life and told him what had happened.

Another time I was driving behind a huge furniture van. A voice said, "You are too close to that. Drop back." I obeyed and the next moment the van put his brakes on full, suddenly, because someone came out from a garage filling station without due care and attention. He drove out straight in front of the furniture van. If I had been nearer I would have driven straight into the back of the van.

In Birmingham, on the Queensway ring road, I was turning right and looking for the traffic coming from the left. There was a van in front with poles, like scaffolding poles, overhanging, but with no warning flag. He was also going right and, as I looked right again, I saw a pole only an inch away from my front windscreen. A broken window would have resulted if I had been an inch farther forward.

On another occasion, I was driving towards a double bend with a bridge over the road. A friend was following me in her car. I thought that, to give her extra warning, I would stab my brakes several times. This slowed me right down. Suddenly a car came fast from the opposite direction. He was over the middle of the road on his wrong side. He would have collided with both of us had we not slowed right down. I thanked God and so did my friend.

Later on God saved me from a road rage attack when I was driving a caravan. On another occasion I mistakenly took a wrong turning. It was as wide as an A road at first but only led to a housing estate.

Because the car park on the estate had an overhead bar to stop large vehicles from entering, I had to turn the nineteen-foot van at a small T junction. I asked the Lord for help, and he sent a young man who was riding a grass cutter. He was willing to drive my car for me whilst I kept a look-out for traffic.

Another time I took a wrong turning it led to a factory whose gates were locked. I again had to turn round at a T junction. I was very hot and tired, so I said, "Lord, you were my pilot when we started this journey so you have got us into this mess. You can get me out of it." His reply was, "You can do all things through me". So I tackled it. While I was manoeuvring, a van driver watched me from a distance. He offered me no help. I stationed Harold on the edge of the pavement into which I was reversing. He waved his arms about for me and I completed the turn, only delaying the other driver for a few minutes. When we arrived home there were 4 cars and a trailer parked so as to prevent me turning into our forecourt. I pulled onto the nearest pavement and unpacked the caravan. When some of the vehicles had gone, I asked Harold to help me. The remaining car was attached to the trailer. However, as I got into my car, the driver of the other vehicle returned. He moved his car and trailer and I asked him, since he was used to towing, if he would reverse our van for me. I told him I was a Christian and had prayed for help as the temperature was in the mid eighties Fahrenheit. He said he was also a Christian and would be glad to help and be the answer to my prayer. He was a decorator who was doing a job for his mother-in-law who lived opposite us.

When we had been at Banbury, we were uncertain as to the best route home. There were three options, two of which I had done many times. I had flunked the third because I knew there was a big roundabout with many exits, some to motorways. This route took us through Warwick instead of Stratford. I started on one of the two I knew well, but found we were going towards Warwick after all. I asked why the Lord chose that way. "You can do all things with my help". I recorded the mileage and time this way. Although the route was five miles longer, the time was the same as shorter routes. It turned out we had avoided gridlocked traffic in Stratford, stuck in the boiling heat. In Stratford there is a road junction without traffic lights. You have to ease your way across several lanes and then back again at the following junction. We heard on the *Midland News* that night that there was a special event at Stratford, and the town was full of people. On the way we actually returned, we had beautiful views and little traffic and did not find the big roundabout a problem. I just "followed my nose" as my father used to say.

**Hiring a caravan**

When Abi was 2½ we heard of Christian camp meetings that were held at a farm at Abbots Lench, only 8 miles from us. We thought we would go and see what they were like. The campers met in a Dutch barn that had bales of straw to sit on and to keep out the draughts. They were very Pentecostal meetings. People brought their own musical instruments to make music to the Lord – tambourines, triangles, drums, violins etc. The speakers were all Evangelical and talked about the gospel of healing. It was "Just up our street." The camp lasted a fortnight in August and was held each year. It was open to anyone, not just to campers and we went for several years as visitors. Later we went as campers.

When Abi was at Primary School she went with her class to visit a small holding whose owner built caravans. When she told us what she had seen we thought about asking if we could hire or buy the one she had described. We agreed to hire it for the August camp and to consider buying it if we liked it. It was a fold-up van, but had a six-foot bath in it that was covered to make a bed. There was also a small kitchen and table and seating and it was entered through a door at the rear end. Other campers advised us not to buy it because home-made vans were not allowed on some sites. However we enjoyed being able to stay at the camp instead of going back and forth for separate meetings.

**Our first caravan: "The Monza"**

My husband went to the Assembly of God Church where the Rev. Eddie Smith was preaching. On Harold's arrival Eddie came across and said, "Hallo mate, how are you? When are you coming to Spitten Camp to stay in camp instead of coming and going?" Harold told him that he had just had a word from God to get a hook put on the back of the car. Harold had mentioned this to me, but I had said, "What do we want a hook for when we have no van and no spare money to buy one?" Oh ye of little faith! Eddie learnt this and said, "Go home and tell your wife, even if she's asleep, to get a hook put on the car. If God has said it you must be obedient. Don't leave it any longer." When Harold got home he came straight to me and told me what Eddie had said. So, next morning, I telephoned Dixon's Garage to ask if they could fit a tow bar to the Allegro Estate Car. They said they could but they would have to strengthen the car. A date was fixed for the job.

When I took the car in I got on a bus to return home but found I did not have the full fare. The money I had would take me to Crab's Cross which was near Hunt End where Harold's parents lived so I decided to go and see them and walk back from there the country lane way.

When I knocked at their door Gran came to answer it and was crying. She said she had just received a letter from her sister, Amy, which said that Amy was to lose a leg from diabetes. She would have to move house to a bungalow and to sell their Monza caravan because she would not be able to use it as the step was too high to get in with only one leg. Also there was no room for a wheel chair. They were going to put the van on the market. I wondered if this were the van God had in mind for us.

I told Harold and we wondered what a Monza van was like. We had no idea about its size or weight. If this were of God the weight must be such that the car could pull it and the size small enough for the mini car space in front of our house. We must also have the money to buy it.

Harold told me to go and see Bill Clark, a caravan owner just up the road. He might know something about Monza vans. Harold knew his Aunt and Uncle had been to Filey Crusades in their van over many years. Abi said she wanted her Daddy to have some money in the post next day for her to believe the van was to be ours.

Bill said he had caravan magazines that we could look at to find weight and size details. Believe it or not, the weight would fit our car and the size was small enough to go in the space we had. We phoned Harold's relatives to ask if we could go to look at it. They agreed and told us they wanted £750 for it. They could not give it away as they needed the money themselves.

There was money in the post next day – £25 for Harold as a gift for his birthday from the Blind Association. The following week end we went to see the van and to have tea. On the way Harold said, "It's going to be bright and light like the sun, gold or yellow colours. When we looked inside it was just as he had described it. The sky-light had a yellow glass so it gave gold light. The cushions were orange and the curtains white daisies on a brown background. There was a gas light over the table and over the bed at the rear. The van had 4 berths, a gas stove, wardrobe, and sink but no toilet or running water. We had a water pump added later and an outside toilet tent with awning. We had trusted God for the money and it came through a forgotten insurance policy that Harold had taken out years before. The £750 was due on his birthday! Harold's Uncle Bernard offered to drive it from Birmingham to our house on Mothering Sunday afternoon, and Bill Clark offered to drive with me on our first trip to give me advice.

Our first trip with the Monza was at Easter 1978 to stay by my parent's house, "The Park". There had been sickness in the family in March and we really wanted a time of relaxation to recuperate. Mother had broken her arm and was glad of some help.

I had an instance of God's protection one day in the Monza. I had put a margarine carton lid down in the cupboard and then put a saucepan down on top of it. When I next put the saucepan on the gas the margarine lid was sticking to the bottom. I did not know this, but, when I lit the gas it burst into flame. I lifted the saucepan to see what had happened and decided to let it burn itself out. It did, but it blackened the whole of the inside of the caravan roof.

When I was new to camping and had the Monza I turned the lever on the jockey wheel so that the van went down to the ground with a bang. (The weight caused the jockey wheel to slide up the groove.) Inside the van was a gallon jar of home-made wine. This was upset and flooded into the carpet so that the van smelt of it for a while. I've never done that again!

**Camping during Huddersfield Dales Week**

We had gone to a show ground near Huddersfield for a Dales Bible Week. It was bed time for Abi but she did not obey the first time I told her to put her things away and get to bed. She was doing some colouring at the table under the gas light. I got cross and said, in a firmer voice, "Will you do as I say and get to bed!" She got up and immediately the gas lamp exploded, shattering splinters from the glass shade all over the place where she had been sitting. If she had not moved, her head might have been cut open.  We praised God for her protection and went into Huddersfield to get a replacement shade, wick and gauze lamp light.

## Caravan Campers Christian Fellowship

At Easter 1979 we promised Mother that we would not go to Llangollen for a Caravan Campers Christian Fellowship holiday.  I had been really ill with 'flu and had nursed others with it also. Mother asked us to stay with her as we had done the previous year. However, in my quiet time God gave me guidance that I would be healed by going to the mountains, and he wanted us to go to the camp.  I phoned my Mother to ask her to release us from our promise.  The result of this was that Mother realised how she had still been trying to rule our lives ever since our marriage, saying we must do this or must not do that.  She apologised when we next saw her and she was very good at keeping her word.  Now I am a mother I have the same tendency and have to check myself from doing the same thing.

## How we became CCCF Members

It is worth telling how we came to be members of the CCCF.  Soon after we acquired the Monza Harold was telling a colleague at work about it.  The colleague was a caravan owner and a Christian himself.  He was a member of CCCF and suggested we might like to try them out and, if we liked them, to join.  He gave Harold an address to write to.

I wrote to their Secretary, Keith Hyden, and back came a booklet with camp sites and details of holidays they run all over the United Kingdom.  The nearest to us was at Clevelode, between Upton-on-Severn and Malvern on 8th September 1978.  We booked to go to this camp as visitors.  I well remember the journey there as it was the first time I had been behind a combine harvester, with traffic queuing behind me.  I decided to overtake when it was safe to do so (though I had memories of saying when I was learning to drive that I would never overtake anything or do more than 30 m.p.h.).

On arrival we were welcomed by a couple parked next to us, Cliff and Val Green.  Val offered us tea to drink and asked where we came from.  This makes such a difference if it is your first visit and you are tired from traffic conditions on the journey.  They told us the

116

time of the evening meeting which was to be in the barn. Cliff was the leader and for his text he used Harold's baptism verse. Harold said, "That's good enough for me to know it is God's will for us to join." We did and are still members 25 years on.

Our caravan was often used to entertain and feed others, to hold prayer meetings and healing services. One Whitsun bank holiday we were in Weston Park when it was very wet all week. Lots of campers went home. Those in a small tent got washed out even though they had dug a trench around the tent. We tried to help them with somewhere warm and dry to eat.

**Our second caravan: "The Cambridge"**

By December 1980, we had changed our Allegro for a Fiat 1600, bought from someone I had known previously. We began thinking it would be nice to have a caravan with a heater inside and a fridge and lavatory. Harold had had a heart attack so double glazed windows would keep in the warmth for him.

At the time we had staying with us Mary Bonham, an old school teacher of Harold's, who was also blind. She had noticed the fire cloth we kept in the Monza to smother any fire on the stove and, as she had recently burnt herself quite badly, she asked if we could take her to buy one for herself. We had bought it at a caravan shop in a place called Kinver, so we decided to go there for another one. As we walked up the path to the shop door, we saw vans for sale with their tow bars facing the path. We peeped through the front window of one which we liked the look of from the outside. I suggested we went inside as the door was not locked. Harold went in first and came out as Mary and I went in exclaiming "Ooh, look, it's got a fridge, a fire, a bathroom and double glazing. Harold was looking at the front and discovered that it had a proper gas chamber inside instead of in a box on the tow bar where the Monza's was. The man in the shop shouted to Harold, "You can't afford that!" Harold replied, "I know I can't but I've just asked my Father for it and he can." The man said the van, a Cambridge, should not have been left open for us to go inside, but as we were obviously interested, he phoned through to the sales office who invited us to go up and discuss the matter over a cup of tea. Mary got her fire cloth from the shop first. We asked the salesman if he would take the Monza in part exchange. He would, and he offered us the same price that we had bought it for, provided it was still in good condition. They

117

would like to come over to see it. The amount we would still have to find was £3,133, but as it was the end of the year and a 1980 model he could knock a bit off the price. We agreed and signed a form for it trusting the Lord for the amount. We told them we would put it all into God's hands.

God gave us all the answers. He said to me, "Go down to the tax office and see what you owe them." I thought there would be some capital gains to pay on some shares I had sold, so I had put money by for that purpose. When they got my papers out, in large letters under "Capital Gains Tax" were the words "No tax owing"; so that set free what I had saved for tax. I was also a beneficiary of a trust which owed me some money. This with savings we had and the £750 allowed for the Monza just made up the price for the Cambridge. So after three weeks we were able to phone the sales office to say that we definitely wanted the van. (Our new car was strong enough to tow a twelve feet eight inch van. The Monza was only ten feet six inches.)

We arranged for the salesman to see the Monza. He was afraid he might get lost, but I said that this would not happen if God were directing this sale. He found his way and was satisfied to purchase it for £750. However, when we told friends from Swindon whom we encountered at a meeting at North Farm in the Cotswolds, about the prospective part-exchange of our Monza for a Cambridge caravan they said they wished they had known. They would have liked to buy the Monza from us as they were finding their old tent "a bit much" now they were older. We had already signed documents in which we had agreed to the part-exchange but I promised to phone the firm to say we had friends who were willing to pay us £750, and would they allow this.

The firm did allow this. In fact they said, "We may be able to do something more for you as we will not have to sell the Monza." They gave us a further discount of £306 which enabled us to purchase gas bottles, a battery, and an awning which incorporated a toilet tent, so we had an inside and an outside toilet.

The Cambridge had fish carved in the edging round the woodwork, and a narrow red line round its middle, which we took to mean the Christian fish symbol and the blood of Christ. Several people remarked on this. There were rose and green cushions, fawn and brown bedding and dark brown curtains and carpet. It seemed darker than the Monza which was the only thing about which I had any reservations.

We collected the new van on March 27<sup>th</sup>, my Father's birthday. When he heard what we had paid for it he thought we were extravagant  It had only cost him £106 when he built "The Ark" caravan and he could only think in hundreds not thousands of pounds. He said, "You're not camping, you're just taking a home from home with all modern conveniences." However we had wonderful holidays in this van for eleven years.

There were many wonderful answers to prayer connected with our purchase. Our special numbers kept coming up. Our daughter, Abi, had predicted that on the day when we would find we had enough money, there would be four letters in the post, and there were four letters that day. It was three weeks from when we first saw the Cambridge until we phoned to confirm purchase. It had taken seven days to negotiate with the salesman to drop the part-exchange so our friends could buy the Monza. We had had it for three years and our friends collected it on 21<sup>st</sup> March, the third month. Three days after we collected the Cambridge our minister came to our house, number 43, to bless the van.

My visitors' book shows that we entertained many people in our new caravan and that people were healed when they had been prayed for there. We went one Easter to a camp for CCCF members at Wellington. On our arrival we found that somehow our jockey wheel had broken. (On another occasion it made a loud banging and fell off!) We asked our friend Cliff Green if he knew anywhere near that we could get it repaired. He said that God had told him to bring his tool kit, including his anvil, for someone at camp who would need it. So he did the repair. What if Cliff had not been obedient to God's request? God can use everyone to meet others' needs if we are all listening and if we follow his instructions.

We have often been offered help by fellow campers, but usually, with God's assistance, we prefer to do things on our own as we know then that they have been done properly. Harold has a firm grip, useful for tightening up. But there have been a few other times when we did need help. Once I got stuck in a gateway. There was a large muck heap nearby and the car was in danger of going into it.

We disconnected the car and moved it, and then several pairs of hands helped us to steer and move the van and reconnect it. (We had to do the same thing without help another time when we turned into a dead end by mistake and had to turn both vehicles round separately.)

At one camp after we had all said "Good night" and gone to our vans I thought it would be nice to put on the Carver gas heater as it was a cold night. For some reason the heater was difficult to light. There was a loud bang. When our neighbour came, because he had heard the bang, he found me on my knees looking to see if the heater was alight. He found the explosion had blown the top off the gas flue. He said, "Are you saying your prayers? I thought you would both have gone to glory by now!"

There had been a time with the Monza when the door would not shut properly and God provided a man with the right tools. I learnt to take screw drivers, spanners, fuses, spare bulbs, string, electric tape, oil WD40, torch, glue, lighter fuel, matches and clothes pegs. All came in useful.

Once, with the Cambridge van, on the way to Banbury, we got stuck on a hill. I was not sure how to engage the four-wheel drive on our new Subaru car. I knew it had to be at a speed below 20 miles per hour. I did not want to cause an accident, so I sent my daughter ahead to warn traffic that was coming down of my hold-up. Lorries and cars came down and then a lorry driver stopped and offered advice, which I followed. So we got to the top and all was well.

**Our third caravan: The "Eccles Elite"**

We had changed our Fiat car for the Subaru 1800. By then the Cambridge van, which had served us for eleven years, began to show wear and tear in its fridge and electrical components. We had been out to lunch with Harold's teacher, Mary Bonham, again but because the Kinver Caravan Centre we went to previously had closed, we decided to go to a caravan sales place in Stourport-on-Severn where we knew somebody. It was his day off, but a nice young lady in the sales office asked what we were looking for and offered to show us round. We said we wanted a two-berth van with six-foot beds that did not have to be put up or down. Now we were older we also wanted to be able to put our feet up for an afternoon snooze. The prices were astronomical – twice what we had paid for our house! We told the lady we wanted to pray and seek God's will on the matter. Two vans interested us. The one had less kitchen and bathroom space, but the bed length and colour scheme were alright. Harold wanted a larger one which was 14 foot 3 inches interior and 19 feet overall. I was not sure about driving this, as it was so much larger than the other one, which was 12 foot 8 inches inside, but only 14 foot 3 inches overall. The sales lady took Mary for a cup of tea and we prayed. Prices were about £6,800 and £11,000. Harold said he was sure God would supply the money and I would regret having a smaller kitchen and shower area. "Remember, every good gift comes from the Father above and if we ask for bread will he give us a stone?" We decided on the larger one if the price could be reduced somewhat. The sales lady said, "Let's look at what we can do. It is now March, 1992, so we can knock off 10% for starters, as the van is a 1991 model and has been on the forecourt for a year." Then she told us what she could give us for the Cambridge. We then asked for special tyres that do not blow out but deflate slowly. She then said she could put a clock in for us free of charge. In the end the price came down from £11,175 to £8,108. We had saved £8,000 from a legacy left to us by my parents who had died in 1986 and 1988.

We agreed to purchase the van, an Eccles Elite, and fixed a date to collect it. On March 27th I changed the insurance and we took the Cambridge over and transferred all the contents from it to the new van. The sales lady said we had restored her faith through her seeing us use our faith and we took her some Full Gospel Business Men's Fellowship International "Voice" magazines. Then we drove to a nearby camp site so that if we had any problems we could get help. The sales lady had said she would come out to the site if needed.

The first problem was that we had forgotten to buy a lock to put on the tow bar to prevent others from taking it away. The warden of the site said thieves had been stealing batteries on their camp so advised us to be sure we locked everything. I therefore went to the telephone box and asked the sales lady to bring us a lock. When we had swapped the vans we had just dumped everything down in the Elite and now I had to sort things and put them away.

Abi, who had got married in 1990, came the first night with her husband to see what we had bought. They helped us learn how new equipment worked. There was central hot air heating, an extra oven and a shower. The next night the sales lady brought the lock for the tow bar. She came with her husband and two boys. They stayed for refreshments and of course we talked about Jesus, not realising what the outcome of our witness would be. A short while later the sales lady was towing an empty caravan. It turned over and so did her car. She immediately sent an arrow prayer to God for help. She came out of it with a whiplash injury to her neck and had to wear a collar for a time. When we heard about this we said we would pray for her. Some things were wrong with our van and she offered to come to collect it from us to get them put right. We said, "May we lay hands upon you for God to heal your neck?" She said, "Yes", so we did so. A week later she brought the van back to us. (When the Stourport place closed we went with the van to their sister shop and centre at Wythall.)

We had not had the new van long when we were asked to loan it for a week as an office for a team who had a crusade in the city. When we went to collect it we were horrified at the state it was in. The toilet was blocked. It had never been emptied. The gas rings on the cooker were dirty, and there were spilt drinks everywhere. The speaker's wife cleaned it for us. However, we decided not to loan it again, even to Christians.

**Angelic Help**

God sent angels to help me on more than one occasion. Once we were going to Minsterley via Shrewsbury when I took a wrong turning. It looked very wide like a ring road, but I found it led to a waste tip and thence into a narrow country lane. I reached a "T"-junction with signposts and stopped to look at the map I always have with me. Just then a tractor came and the driver asked if he could help. I told him where I wanted to be and he said he would turn the car and van around if I watched out for traffic. (I explained that Harold was blind so could not help.) No other traffic came down the lane so we were able to go back and then on to the correct turning.

**Flooded Ford**

Another time, when driving to Wellington, I took a turning too soon, but saw a big garden centre on the right with a car park where I thought I could turn round. However, when I asked they refused and told me I could get to the village by going on down the road I was on. They did not tell me I would have to cross a ford to get there. I drove on and saw the sign, "Ford Ahead" so I went to see how deep it was. Ducks were swimming happily on it! We had been having a lot of rain and it looked too fast and deep to go through and I did not know if the base was hard or soft. There was no one to ask. I went to report back to Harold that I would have to back for at least three quarters of a mile. I went to see if the road was clear behind and found a white car waiting for me to move on. I reported the flooded river ahead. The driver said, "I'm used to backing a car with a boat behind, would you like me to back this up to the farm gate and turn round there?" I thanked him and said he was an angel sent from God. He said he was pleased to help, and did so. Then he went on his way.

## Toilet problems

At the Thame CCCF Spring Bank Holiday, Harold went with me to empty the toilet into the Elsan pit. I can do this with a trolley or truck, but often the lids on the tanks are too heavy for me to lift. This time the tank was near a barbed wire fence and as Harold was replacing the lid he lost his balance and swung his arms in an attempt to save himself from falling. He slashed his arm and writs on the fence. It was more than a sticking plaster job so we went to the camp's first aid tent. They said we should go to the local cottage hospital near Oxford. We were treated in the out-patient department there. We did some witnessing at the Hospital so the time was not wasted. The whole camp prayed for Harold as the news spread around. Not a single scar was left when the bandages were removed. (The dog had a holiday, as Harold could not feel the harness when the bandages were on. After that the top to the septic tank was changed so that others would not come to similar harm.)

At another camp we were carrying a toilet container when someone made a joke about Harold going to the "Ladies". He dropped his end of the container, and that caused me to lose my balance. To save myself I also let go of the container and I hit a concrete wall that was studded with stones. My glasses were severely scratched but in the spot near where the ear-piece is connected, so I did not have to buy a new pair.

## Movers and Shifters

One day, when at Top Barn with the Worcester Anglican Renewal Ministries, we noticed that campers in the next pitch to ours had a mover fixed to their van because the owner had severe back problems. We watched them as they prepared to leave, using the mover to bring the van to the car tow bar. There was no lifting, pushing, or pulling involved. Harold and I thought, "That's just what we need at our age." (We were then 65 and 73.) We inquired of the friend up the road who had helped us with the Monza. He had just had a *Caravan Magazine* with an article on movers, which he brought for us to read. There were two articles, one on movers and one on shifters. The mover is put onto the van, but the shifter is battery operated and stored on a trolley. It has to be stored when not in use. It is also difficult to transport.

We had enough money saved to buy a mover, so I phoned our nearest caravan centre. They said they had just one left in stock. If I took my eleven-year-old van to them they would see if the mover could be fitted to it. The price was £995. We fixed August 5$^{th}$ as we were going away on August 10$^{th}$. This would give me time to empty the van and to get the money transferred.

In case the chassis of the Eccles could not take the mover, the salesman suggested we should look at their modern vans. This was a new possibility.

I went to the Lord in prayer. It seemed as though all systems were "GO" for a new van. The Centre thought our Eccles van was worth £1,000 to £1,500. We could sell it in part-exchange, as we had done with the Cambridge. However, as we thought of the value of the Eccles, we wondered if it might be better to give it away. We knew where it would be accepted with open arms. We had already bought three caravans and three tents so that other people could have Christian camp holidays for their families. When we bought the Eccles I had felt that God had plans for it to be passed on to other Christians after we had finished with it.

Our stockbrokers had sent us some money, which would allow us to make a purchase. So we went to look at the new vans but were not impressed. There were none that we liked as much as the one we had. There was always something wrong with the lay out, or colour, or price, or size, or weight.

We had previously considered a Caravette (camper van) and had looked at different makes of these that friends used. Three facts put us off them. When you are away you have to pack up things inside if you want to drive from the site for shopping. Car parks in towns are not always convenient for vehicles of a camper van's height. You may need extra equipment to ensure the Caravette is level if the ground is sloping or uneven on the campsite. Nevertheless, we went to a place in Evesham where they made them, but found only a security guard. He said he did not have keys to any of the vehicles but we could look at the exteriors and through the windows. We had no urge to see inside.

The caravan centre phoned to say they could fit the mover, but it would not allow much clearance to go over speed bumps (then known as "sleeping policemen"). The mover would be powerful enough to work on a gradient of 20% so it should easily cope with the hill at home.

**Seeking God's will**

I was still wondering what the God's will was. I had a reading which said that God can give you the solution to every problem. If you choose to follow your own agenda instead of his, don't be surprised if things go wrong. Let God be in control. Bring your disturbed feelings to him. He provides good things that pass man's understanding if we love him. In church the sermon was about the children of Israel who had forgotten to depend entirely on the Lord for their existence. They had to re-establish that connection again. God is the source of our supply. Allow him to work. God is the prime mover and requires our co-operation and commitment. Move forward and be involved in his world. Listen to his Spirit for direction each day. Don't make impetuous decisions that are not carefully thought through. An impulsive act could be from your own spirit, not his. Share with others what you think God is saying to you. I shared all this with Harold.

Next in the readings was a caution from the story of Jonah. Things can look alright and yet be all wrong. When God says "No" he ceases to keep you in his hands and leaves you to act in your own strength. You find that insufficient. When God's anointing is removed it leads to breakdowns, all sorts of pressures and shut doors. Do not try to open them. If it is God's "Yes" all will go easily and be successful. Stay at the level where you can cope. If you don't know what to do, then fast and pray. He will supply energy and materials. There is no need to worry or lose sleep or peace of mind. There will be no failures.

After reading this advice I decided to go over the events so far.

A mover would not have entered our minds if we had not seen one on a van parked next to us

There was the article in the magazine we were given to read

The Caravan Centre could fit one

We had the money for it.

These were all signs to go ahead. On the other side was the fact that we had no peace of mind and lost sleep weighing up the pros and cons of different ideas. We had managed from 1978 until 2002 without a mover.

**Keeping the Eccles and buying a mover**

We took the Eccles to the Caravan centre. We had an easy hook-up and clear drive and were there before they opened. We agreed they should fit the mover and we would collect the van five days later.

The caravan people phoned to say that the tyres on the Eccles were worn as they had done over 4,000 miles. The Centre had tyres available. Should they put them on? We agreed so long as they were the same as the old ones.

When we returned to collect the Eccles I was feeling a bit nervous as I am inclined to be a little forgetful when under the stress of using anything new (even kitchen equipment). My readings had said that if feeling nervous one should just speak the name "Jesus". This ensures the retreat of the enemy and his evil forces. When you are no longer anxious, speak the name of Jesus in thankfulness that he's brought you through.

The men arrived and we went to the office to pay. They had put the van outside in the parking area. I asked for tuition on how to use the mover and the girl who took the money came out with us to show me the process.

They had pumped up the tyres to 45 units of air-pressure to give extra clearance. The lady attached the lever to engage the mover – "Front to rear to engage and rear to front to release". I got that. "Then use the remote control to move in different directions, by pressing the button." Well, it stopped after 2 yards because the battery was flat. I had known it was low and had asked them to

126

recharge or replace it. They had not done so. We had to buy another battery and bring the old one back to recharge on our charger. After the lady had shown me the ropes I did the exercise for myself. A man came with the new battery and I asked the lady to hook up while I went to their shop to buy a tyre pressure gauge. I asked the two of them when I returned if they had checked the doors were locked and the mover inside, so I did no further checks.

We started out but soon after, at a roundabout, I could not see or hear if the direction indicator lights were working. (We were driving our 4th Subaru car and I thought the flashing signs might be different or the car radio too loud to hear the indicator sounds) The car also felt very different with the extra weight and I needed more brake-power. Four miles and two turns later we reached home. I went to remove the electrical connections, but I found the firm had never attached them. I had thought they would have known how to attach a caravan to a car so I had not checked up on them.

Previously I would have backed onto our drive, but as we now had the mover I stopped the car in the road (which sloped downhill). We took the stabiliser off and it was very difficult to disconnect the ball and bar with the weight pulling backwards. I was in front watching for traffic and parked cars. When we did succeed in disconnecting, the van started to run away, so I called to Harold to put on the brake. He was not in a position to do so, as he was facing the wrong way, holding the handle on the socket. It became obvious we could not stop the van which was gaining speed. I thought the best thing was to steer it into the kerb, but the pumped-up tyres jumped the kerb. When the jockey wheel reached the kerb, and the van wheels were on the softer ground of our neighbours' lawn, it stopped with a *big jolt*.

Harold went into the house to get himself a brandy for the shock while I phoned a friend up the road to see if he could help. By the time he arrived the mobile library had come and the driver asked if he could help. The two men lifted the jockey wheel up onto the pavement. I put on the mover and steered the van along on the pavement (which was wide enough to take it). I parked it in our drive as easily as anything.

Fortunately, the neighbours were away at the time, and, miraculously, when they returned, they could not see where the wheels had been. It was also a miracle that I turned the van into the kerb when I did as it just missed a wall round our garden which would have damaged the van if I had turned it any sooner. As it was holiday time it was also a miracle that no children were about on their bikes or skateboards, and that no one was pushing a pram on the pavement.

A neighbour opposite had watched all this. She did not know we had had a mover and wondered why we were running down the road after our van instead of putting it in our drive. We had our lunch and a well-deserved rest before I went out to reload the Eccles with everything I had removed before taking the van to the caravan centre. I was amazed to hear bubbling sounds in the van's water system, and I mentioned this to Harold. We found out why on the first day of our holiday.

We put the old battery on charge to be ready for use later, and I also found a small solar charger we had used before, so I put that in the van for use, as I realised how much the mover could deplete a battery.

**Trusting technology rather than the Lord**

In my quiet time after the van ran away I asked the Lord why all this had been allowed to happen. The answer was, "Because you put your trust in, and got help from, machinery instead of direct from me. Before this you relied on my help entirely and it has been given to you all along." Next morning my readings confirmed my message from God. He opposes pride and self-confidence and relying on our own resources instead of on him. God means what he says and does what he declares.[30] Depend on him in every situation in which you find yourself and deepen your trust in him. Know God's "stops" as well as his "starts". If he tells us to stop, we can make a fuss and complain and argue and go in the opposite direction from his, or we can wait with a growing trust that he does all things well. How do we prepare for what we're not yet ready, except by trusting God?

My prayer to the Lord was, "I get your message, but please may we go on this week's holiday as everything is now ready." I did not feel happy in my spirit because I knew that without God's "Yes" and his

---

[30] Amos 6: 8 and Isaiah 55:11

128

anointing all sorts of things could happen; if our action were "of the flesh", it could not do us any good. I was washing up the dishes and word came, "You can go, but on your own head be it." I felt so disturbed I could not concentrate on what I was doing. I said to Harold, "I want two friends who live up the road to come down and pray with us, just to get another Christian to confirm or otherwise. I phoned them and, though it was Saturday, they came straight away. (It was an answer to prayer.)

I explained to them all that I felt was guidance from the Lord, as were the "stop" and the "go" signs. We went into the lounge to pray. They both came up with the same answer. It was right to go. The enemy was putting fear in my heart to stop us. They knew our ministry and hospitality for other campers and the meals we gave them in our van. Harold also felt the "Go" was stronger than the "no". I thought here were three witnesses who agreed and my confidence returned. I put the last food items and table and chairs in the van. Later my friends drove round in their car to see if we were going. I said, "Yes". My energy and strength had returned to cope.

**Our holiday using the mover**

We had an easy hook-up and departure for our holiday at Spitten Farm. When we reached the campsite we found the driveway had been flattened at the entrance especially for us in answer to a request I'd made. We parked in our usual place at the rear of the barns. While we were unhooking a man from another van came to greet us. He and his wife had arrived the previous night having driven all the way from Devon. They were in their late eighties. We made friends straight away and looked after them and took them shopping. We shared meals and prayer in the van and took them to see our home during the week.

One day after lunch, before seeing to the waste water and loo, I fetched the water roll, plugged it into the intake, switched on the pump and opened the taps on the basin and sink to get rid of an air lock. No water came through! Harold said he could hear water flowing into one of the bedding lockers. I rushed to switch off the pump before looking to see if he was right. He was! Pillows and bedding were all wet. It was a hot day so I put them out on chairs in the wind and sun and before nightfall they were dry. But we could not use the pump for the week. Instead we used water carriers and cans which we humped by hand as we had had to do in the Monza before a pump was installed. The difference was that I was now 73 not 50 years old.

The next day was also very sunny so I put both the solar chargers on. We had our Devon friends in to high tea and then went to the evening meeting in the barn. We forgot to unplug the chargers before we left, and half an hour later the sun went down. The solar rays were no longer strong enough to charge the battery. When we returned, three hours later, I opened the van door and was hit by a terrible smell of burning! I put the light on and started where the smell was strongest by the fridge. I saw the plug was red hot and pulled it out of its socket. I followed the cable wire to the sun charger. It had slipped behind a cushion and had melted the covering of the wire and for over a foot it had melted the cushion, curtain, and bed cushion to a dark brown colour. I was glad the material was non-flammable. The cushions bore the text, "Where two or three are gathered together in my name, there am I in the midst."[31] The Lord said it was the written word that saved us from fire. It was Jesus, not the material, saved our caravan from going up in smoke. More praise and thanks to God.

The battery was also drained, instead of charged. On further inspection I found there was a break in the wire in the charger cable. This was the cause of the over-heating and melting. So I used torches at night and invited people round in the daytime instead of after dark.

All had a wonderful week! We helped with hospitality and contributed to the gathered family in prayer, praise and Bible study, and in other get-togethers. We felt refreshed in body, mind and spirit.

We returned home after a very good journey and parked on the road. I got the mover on but found the battery was too low to move it. We had left a charger on in the house so I rushed to get the battery. I was just swapping them when, lo and behold, a huge lorry with bricks and a crane came down the road. He said he had taken a wrong turn but would back out without waiting for me to finishing moving the van into our drive.

---

[31] Matthew 18:20

We phoned our friend, Alan, who services the van, to see if he could stop the water leaking into the locker before our next camp, booked for September 2002. A few days later he came and took out the whole water tank. We had broken a part, which probably could not be replaced, given the age of the van. He therefore made it so that the water did not go into the tank at all but straight from the water roll to the taps. This was no great loss as we had only once used the shower and hot water tank.

**Seeking God's will again**

We had to cancel a camping holiday in Evesham so Harold could train with a new dog. I began to wonder whether this was a further sign from God to let this be the last season for us to use the caravan. But, after my daily readings, there were thoughts to the contrary. Just because something is difficult and takes time and effort it does not necessarily mean it is not right. If something is right it is still possible. If something is in God's will it is not only possible but worth every minute, every pound of money and every ounce of energy we expend. Problems we face are opportunities for us to show the world that we really are children of God and over-comers. God's glory is squeezed out like juice from an orange when we trust him under pressure. Through hard times God can show us aspects of his nature we would never know otherwise, and also expose us to his glory. When something is over, you will know it. When you have tried to make something work and it has not worked, then you accept his will in the matter. We are told in the book of Job not to look to anything or anyone except God to meet our needs. God's gifts are tools to manoeuvre you to where you can fulfil his purposes and have greater influence. The enemy is not just after your provision but also your purposes. When God gives you something, he puts you on an assignment to use it for his glory. When you receive your provision, read the instructions that go with it! His instructions were to go to campsites to preach the Good News to all manner of people who would not otherwise hear it. Take the Gospel to the unsaved. The only qualification God needs in his servants is that we should know and admit our own inadequacy and watch out for the counterfeit. We must stand firm in the faith, resist the enemy and he will flee. So I "put the van to bed" while awaiting God's further instructions.

The following year I received the answers my prayers for guidance. If God willed me to travel with the van, other people would talk about it to me. Two days later our stockbroker was on the phone and asked if we had already been away. Then Diana, my sister, phoned and left a message on our answer phone. When I returned her call she told me she thought we might have been away. Then a friend phoned to ask if we had booked for any CCCF camp yet. Three people had spoken about it in that week. My answer!

(We asked our friend Alan to service our van the next day. Harold and I then spring-cleaned the inside, polishing the woodwork with beeswax. I hosed down the outside. This needed a lot of "elbow grease" to remove the green slime.)

My daily reading asked the question, "Have you learnt your lesson?" If so, God is a God of second chances. He has promised to journey with us and protect us from harm. He is committed to escorting his people to the end of their journey. It may not be all hunky dory, but his presence will help us cope with any fear or danger. What you are going through now is preparation for the future.

The Bible is full of people going on journeys. What do you do when you make a "wrong" decision yet come to the same one a second time round? It's easy to let the past cripple the future through fear we might "blow it" again. But God has more grace and more confidence in us, and our ability to learn. Jonah learnt from his past decision-making. He was told to go to Nineveh for three days[32], so I thought this indicated we should go to a city camp for three days. I wrote off for a booking form for a Caravan Campers Christian Fellowship camp near Banbury.

However, a friend's daughter phoned to ask if we knew the dates of the Worcester Anglican Renewal Ministries camp that year for her parents wanted to go. She asked if we would be there. Then a newsletter arrived with dates of Spitten Farm camp events for the year. So there were lots of possibilities. The only possible negative sign was that as I had done too much spring-cleaning and gardening, my muscles went into spasm and my back hurt. This was painful

---

[32] Jonah 3:3

and limiting but I was sure that, as I had received much prayer, I would be better by the time we would go away.

**More camping in the Eccles van**

We were still using the Eccles Caravan, but we did not use the mover again. I discovered we had the wrong sized battery to meet the demands of a mover, and we could not have a larger battery as the space in the van was not big enough for one

However we did not take the mover off the van. A gentleman came to the house when the van was parked there and offered us £2,000 in cash for the van and the mover. I declined his offer, saying that, when we were ready to part with it, other Christians would have it. He said he himself was a Christian, and he came back some months later to see if we had changed our minds. We had not.

In the four years since then we have had many more holidays with the CCCF and WARM camps. The van developed more faults during this time in the toilet and water systems, cupboards and door, and the turning light signals were very unreliable. However God made sure there was always help at hand when things went wrong.

In May 2006, we were at a spring bank holiday rally. One of the members on site had learnt that we had problems with a brand new battery we had bought for our Easter holiday that year. He was fully trained in electrical matters and he tested the electrical system for the car and the van to determine that the battery was flat. I had left our charger at home, thinking we should not need it as the battery was new, so our electrician friend connected his and left the battery on charge for 24 hours. Within 2 hours, the battery was flat again so we had to take it back. The place where we bought it made us pay for another battery until they had had time to check out the one we had returned, but a week later they phoned to offer us a refund.

That holiday was the wettest, muddiest and coldest May bank holiday we had experienced in 27 years of camping. The dog was the colour of chocolate, although I took bin liners for him to lie on. The inside of the marquee was inches deep in mud. Even though the organisers asked campers not to use their cars into or out of the site, I had to drive across it because the site was too big for Harold to walk the whole way across, as he had mobility problems.

Hot weather was a great help in drying five loads of washing, so I was able to store away the caravan linen for the winter.

After the turn of the century we had more years of camping. We made more friends and helped more people.

At one camp the BBC came to film the daughter of the camp's warden, Eve, for the series *"Child of our Time"*. Eve wanted to see Harold's dog, Uska, so we were filmed too. Abi later saw the programme, and phoned to say, "Mum you're on Television." They showed me as I was returning from the septic tank, with bottles in my hand for our water supply. I saw myself with Eve and Uska and the film crew filming.

In September 2006 I told friends at CCCF that I would cancel my membership at the end of the year because I felt it would be difficult with my health problems to carry on for another year of camping. However, in March 2007 I felt I badly needed a holiday, so in faith I rejoined CCCF. The battery for the van had been on charge each month since the previous September, but the man who serviced the van found a fault in the charger. He put it right, so when booking forms came with the March newsletter of the Caravan Campers, I asked for God's guidance on whether we should book for the May bank holiday. I would count mention of *holidays*, *camp*, or *journey* as a sign we should go.

He gave me three signs to go ahead. When I was phoning our stockbroker he asked me if we were going away in our van that year for Easter, but I said we were thinking of the Spring Bank *Holiday*. The second sign was that my daily readings mentioned the *journey* made by Abraham's servant to find a wife for Abraham's son, Isaac. The third sign was another reading that spoke of how the Israelites stayed in *camp* after they were circumcised.[33]

We were all ready for the final packing on 24th May. We did not have to leave early, since the organisers needed until 11.00 a.m. to prepare for the arrival of 200 caravans. We had an easy hook-up and I did not need to ask the owners of parked cars to move them so we could get out of our driveway. The journey would be 68 miles, so I checked everything and asked for God's help and for the protection of angels for our house during our absence. En route I made one mistake in direction and went into an industrial estate, but someone

---

[33] Genesis 24: 10-11 and Joshua 5: 8

told us the way from there and we were soon on the right road again. To guide us on the last lap there were CCCF signs.

People were posted at the gate to hand us a map of the camp site and the spot allotted to us. This was near the hub tent and would be noisy. I had asked for a quiet spot on the booking form. They told us someone had cancelled so we could have a spot directly opposite the entrance, so it would be ideal for Abigail to find us next day when she was due to visit us. It was also on high ground at the top of a slope. Little did we know how blessed we were because, after two sunny days, there was continuous rain for two days and a night. The lower part of the site became waterlogged and four-wheel drive vehicles had to tow late arrivals to their patches. When the farmer asked campers not to drive on site I decided to stay put for 10 days. It was a rest for me not to be driving and the dog liked it too as there was hard ground nearby where I could exercise him four or five times a day. I fed him and took him to the dog walk area between 5.00 a.m. and 6.00 a.m. each day. Then I had my breakfast and quiet time and had to give Harold an insulin injection at 7.15 a.m. There was a daily prayer meeting at 8.00 a.m. and about 22 people braved the cold, wet, mud to be there.

There was a friend in the next caravan whom we had known for nine years. He lent us a clothes line so that I did not have to hang wet things from the bars of the roof rack on our car. Later the organisers put a heater in a tent for campers to dry things, but some campers whose beds had been soaked when water got into their tents, went home.

God provided for our needs. My track suits hung on our friend's line and later could air in our van. There was a site shop that stocked all we needed. Because Harold could not walk to the hub tent, the consecrated bread and wine from the Pentecost Communion were brought to him. Friends often came to talk to him.

Bank Holiday Monday was one of the very wet days. The organisers provided a covered play area for children where they could bounce on inflated mattresses. For adults there was an indoor "car-boot" sale for which you had a space for your own table if you paid £3. I took my table across on a sack wagon we used for our water carrier. God provided a man to tow it across the field for me as I had two bags of greetings cards and other things to sell and had a job to keep everything dry. The greetings cards were ones I had recycled for our church funds and at 20p each I made a profit that day of £7!

At camp, you make new friends and you hear of others who have troubles that are worse than your own: children on drugs, family members with cancer, encephalomyelitis, leukaemia or other illnesses. God gave me encouragement when the man who lent us the clothes line said, "If anyone at camp deserves a gold medal it is you!" Also, a lady said in the prayers of thanksgiving, "Thank you, God, for Harold and Jo." This was quite unexpected, but I learnt later that I had been an inspiration to other ladies who said, "If Jo can do it, I can!" I thank God that we can be examples without knowing that we are being watched and copied.

On the last day, a Sunday, there was a communion service before everyone packed up. We got our car to the van and managed to hitch up. However, I had to get help from someone to fit the stabiliser. Then, on the drive, I saw the passenger wing mirror had been knocked away from its proper position. I stopped to correct this and realised I was not sure of the way out. We were able to follow another car. However, when we had gone some miles the Holy Spirit reminded me that I had not checked if the screw on the stabiliser had been tightened. I stopped as soon as it was safe to do so and found the screw was missing altogether! When I looked in the boot of the car I found the screw was still there. It had never been put in! If I had attached the stabiliser myself I would have noticed this before leaving the field. As we had done a number of left and right turns the stabiliser and van might have come adrift. Angels must have protected us. Things went smoothly for the rest of the way.

# CHAPTER ELEVEN: HOLIDAYS

## 1973, Lindley Lodge Christian Centre

Nineteen-seventy-three saw us going on our first holiday since Abi's birth. We went to Lindley Lodge near Nuneaton. It was run by Torch Fellowship for the Blind. We received God's guidance to go there in three ways. Firstly, we could not attend a clinic at Shrewsbury. Secondly, we did not book when first told about it, but asked God to get the same person who had approached us to invite us a second time if it was his will for us, which they did. Thirdly there were still vacancies.

At Lindley Lodge we were in a room with three single beds and I remember going from one to the other several times during the night. While there we had our first experience of street evangelism, going down into town where I gave my testimony with a loud-haler.

## 1974, Whatcombe Christian Centre

The success of our holiday at Lindley Lodge led us to go to Whatcombe House the following year for the week's holiday at Pentecost. It was led by the Reverend Reginald East. There were talks on the Holy Spirit, how the Apostles preached in the power of the Holy Spirit with all boldness, leading to signs and wonders. It was the kind of teaching that added people to the Church. These early Christians suffered persecution and they moved on to different nations. It is the work of the Holy Spirit to bring people to maturity.

On one of the free afternoons we went to a nearby town and bought our daughter a toy tractor that was propelled along by a child's legs. It was too big to go inside the car so we put it on the roof.

## Cropthorne

The first time I visited *Holland House*, the Retreat House for Worcester Diocese was when a retreat was being run there by the Mothers Union. Though I was not a member, this led to my being invited to be put on their speakers' list and that led to my talking on healing at their meetings. The courage part of my baptism verse was used to arrange a gathering of local ministers, "Be strong and of a good courage; fear not for the Lord thy God doth go with thee"[34]. The Rev. R. Neil taped a talk for them about healing work in the Anglican ministry. I look back on that year. What a lot was packed

---

[34] See footnote 13

in! Life was exciting. Who would have believed so much would be seen and learnt and so many openings provided by God for growth.

**Two Prophecies**

When Mary and Alex Learmont came to stay with us in the early nineteen eighties, Mary said to me, while we were together in the kitchen preparing lunch, "Jo, You will be going to the U.S.A." I replied that I did not think this was likely as my travelling days were over. I thought nothing more about what Mary had said until, in 1996, Abi and her husband, Paul, were going to spend 6 months in America in connection with his work. They invited us to stay with them while they were there. As usual, I prayed, asking God if it was in his plan for us. Then the Holy Spirit reminded me of Mary's prophetic word all those years earlier. I took this reminder as God's answer that we should fulfil that prophecy. Abi and Paul had been in the United States from January until April, and then they returned to England for just a week. They would travel with us as they were going back at the end of that week. So it was good that we would not have to travel alone. We were given plenty of time to prepare, so I wrote to the Headquarters of the Full Gospel Business Men's Fellowship International to find out if there was a branch near where Abi and Paul were living.

In reply to my letter to the American headquarters, a reply came back with an invitation for us to attend a morning meeting on a Sunday in the office of a factory that was not far from where Abi was then living. Abi took us to the place, but did not stay. I said I would find the right door and room and then return for Harold. I entered the premises and announced myself to the steward at the door. He went to get the Minister from his room which was like a vestry. The minister welcomed me with a big hug, and I hugged him in return. He then shouted to the congregation, "It's all right folks, she's one of us." I then fetched Harold and we were shown to their wash room to freshen up. The Pentecostal Sunday Service was wonderful, with singing in tongues, prophecy and words of knowledge. There were children present, and one of them, a nine-year old, asked if she could prophesy over us. We agreed to this. She said, "You can reach the hearts of strangers, but you cannot reach your own family. God has taken you through ups and downs.

He has stretched you and relaxed you like a rubber band." (The "stretching" represents to us the testing we have experienced, while the "relaxing" represents the times of blessing.) The child's prophecy continued, "God says, trust your family to me. Just live out your life before them. Don't try to convert them now." When Abi returned with Paul, the Minister came out to see us leave. He said to Abi, "You have got very Godly parents", to which she replied, "I haven't got them, they have got me".

We had a wonderful weekend trip with Abi and Paul to see the Niagara Falls, an awesome sight! We wanted to go to Toronto to find the Toronto Airport Christian Fellowship, famed in 1994 for the "Toronto Blessing". This church later became the subject of much controversy, but, at the time, we wanted to find out about the revival there. No one at our hotel, or at a taxi rank where we asked to be taken there, had ever heard of it, so we took this as a "No" from God, and did not seek any further.

**Pembroke, Canada**

In 1999 we went to a Family Reunion in Canada. One of my Father's cousins had had four daughters who married Canadians at the end of the Second World War. Their husbands had been members of the armed forces who had been stationed in England. They and their descendants met for reunions every three years and we were invited, along with my sister. Previously, I had suffered from air sickness when the air was turbulent. I prayed for calm this time, and God answered my prayer by sending me to sleep. I stayed asleep when the plane hit a rough patch.

By this time the Canadian family numbered about a hundred persons and booked camping sites, but we were put up in a nearby motel. At the camp site, different branches of the family took it in turns to cook lunch and supper for everyone. There was a river near the site that flowed through Pembroke, and a path beside the river. My husband, Harold, and I walked along this path, and then took a sight-seeing tour of the town in an open tourist train. Soon after the tour, when we had got back to the footpath, Harold was suddenly taken ill. He was already a diabetic, so I always carried sugar sweets with me. I gave him one, and he sat down on a public seat nearby. I knew he would not be able to walk back to the camp, so I said, "I will go to find someone with a car to drive you back." As I walked I prayed to God, asking him to send someone to be company for Harold, so he would not be left alone in a strange place. A member of our family agreed to drive to collect him. When we reached him there was a crowd standing round him. He was amusing them by telling them all his jokes. He had recovered completely. Prayers are answered every day. The more you give thanks for the answers, the more you see and recognise. Because there is sometimes a delay between the request and the answer, when the answer does come the request may have been forgotten.

## CHAPTER TWELVE: SICKNESS
**Ill health in the year we were married.**
At the end of 1968, my husband and I both had influenza, in my case linked to residual problems with the occult. However, we prayed with thankful hearts for all God had done, though I still had an unsolved health problem. When Harold prayed about it he was given a revelation of a red flower. All its petals were separate, like tongues of flame. Suddenly all the flames came together to form the flower. It became a rose of Sharon. A gynaecologist with whom I had an appointment could find nothing wrong with me. Praise the Lord!

### 1969 Mother's Heart Attacks and Pneumonia
In January, I went to my mother's home as was my weekly practice. I was very surprised to be met at the door by my Aunt Mary who lived nearby. She said Mum had had "one of her turns". Dad had gone to a National Farmers Union meeting and he had asked my aunt to sit with Mum until I arrived. It was evident she had had a loss of memory; since she said, "I don't know why I am in bed. Why am I?" I told her she had had a turn like one she had had some years before.

This time she had been weeding a rockery with her arms above her head, something she should not have done. I told her she must rest and I would stay with her. I prayed for Harold to phone me so I could ask him to get onto the prayer chain for support. The verdict this time was also a heart attack and it took 3 men 7 hours praying before she was back to normal. I am sure the prayers helped. I was able to leave her and go home when Dad returned.

In 1978 Mother had a fall and broke her arm. However, she insisted on going to Eastbourne, where my Father and she had spent their honeymoon, and to which they frequently returned. She had been invited to visit a niece who lived there, and did not want to disappoint her. She and my Father called on me two days before they left, and I had a premonition that I would not see Mother alive again. I therefore posted a book for her on things we often fail to say to loved ones while they are alive. On their arrival, Mum asked Dad to "find a letter from Jo". Dad said, "We've only just seen her", but he asked for any post at hotel reception and found my letter and book. While in Eastbourne, Mother developed pneumonia, the words in the book kept her fighting for her life. Her niece had to drive my parents back home. She was very ill for a long time. On her birthday in October of that year she said to me, "I wish they would let me go! I don't want to live if I cannot look after Dad. Please don't revive me again."

I asked several friends to pray about this and hoped this was a decision we would never have to make. In fact, she began making progress to full recovery, and lived for nine more years.

When Mothers' Day came round the next year, I asked a friend to make a card for her using pressed flowers. To make the card more personal, I wrote a poem:

> "To have you with us on Mothers' Day,
> is proof God answers, when we pray.
> To say how much we love you, Mum,
> I've had this card of flowers done.
> The larkspur and lobelia, dried,
> tell of the summers' days of sun
> and hope for the summer yet to come.
> We know not yet the days we'll see,
> but know you will live eternally."

## Harold's Viral Fibrositis

One morning early Harold woke up feeling dreadful, aching all over, and unable to lift his head. I thought it might be rheumatic fever, but the doctor we called diagnosed it as viral fibrositis. He gave us a prescription for pain killers and a note for a week off work. Harold was to keep warm and take care of himself and all would be well. It was a great opportunity for me to read books to him. Don Basham's "Face Up With a Miracle"[35] was just the subject to help our faith to believe in Harold's healing. So was one of Smith Wigglesworth's books.[36] We felt so inspired by them that Harold said he was healed and he got up to go back to work saying, "If we believe in healing, why am I in bed?"

He was still in pain when he got dressed and walked to the bus. There he witnessed to others in the queue that God had healed him whereupon the pain left him and by the time he got to his work place he felt fine. Believe it has already happened and it will be so. Harold stepped out in faith and God honoured it.

---

[35] Face Up with a Miracle, Whitaker House, 1967
[36] Faith that Prevails, Bibliotheca di Evangelo, 1938

## An Osteopath

At the end of the year we had a letter from a friend, named Lucy, saying she'd read in a newspaper of an osteopath who worked in Shrewsbury bringing sight back to blind people by cranial massage. Lucy posted the item, cut from the paper, to us as she thought we would be interested to see if he could help Harold regain his sight. We, of course, took it to the Lord in prayer, asking for his guidance on the matter. Harold got information on osteopaths in Shrewsbury from the library in Redditch. We asked the Lord, if it was his will for Harold to go for this treatment, that we should pick the right name from the list of names that Harold had been given. (A relative had given us some money. She said she would rather help us in time of need than leave us £150 in her will later.)

From the list of names and telephone numbers, I selected one, Brooks, which I rang in the evening, about 7.00 p.m. A lady answered and I said we had read a newspaper article about an osteopath who brought sight back to the blind, and did we have the right number. She said, "Yes". Later she told us that she had gone back to the practice after hours to clear up a mess left by painters and decorators. At first she thought she need not answer the phone as it was out of hours, but had second thoughts about how she might wonder who it was if she did not pick up the receiver. God again!

We arranged for an interview because Mr. Brooks was such a busy man, that he would only take on people he felt sure could be helped. When we saw him he said to Harold, "You're just up my street. I'm sure I can help you, but first I want you to visit an endocrinologist to check on the state of your glands and blood supply.

An appointment was made to see a Mr. Capewell in Harbourne, Birmingham. We went in January 1972. Mr. Capewell explained what he was going to do and why he needed to do it. He asked Harold how he lost his sight and then put a collar over his thyroid. Using a spectroscope he could tell, from colour change in the blood after 3 minutes irradiation, what work the gland was doing. While Harold was on the machine he looked hard at me and asked if I minded if he took my pulse rate. I said I did not as long as he did not charge me for doing so! He said my pulse rate was only 56 beats a minute instead of 72 and then told me my whole medical history which was correct in every detail. He said any offspring would be sufferers from eczema and asthma. (Our daughter Abigail had both of those.) He spoke of the problems connected with my pregnancy and delivery which were also right. He outlined my own problems as slow digestion, slow elimination, piles, heartburn, hiccups, poor periods, and dry skin and lips. In fact I needed treatment more than my husband otherwise I would have more problems, such as fibroids at the menopause.

All this came as a shock as it doubled the expense. My parents said they would look after Abigail on the days we went to Shrewsbury and we could leave her with Harold's parents sometimes when we went to Mr. Capewell.

We were praying about the added treatment when the day's calendar reading was "Go forward to meet your good." This was good enough for me. (The calendar was a Christmas present for which we had Mrs. Babs Honey to thank.)

We told others at church about these events and four other people had similar needs and asked if we could take them with us for consultation and treatment if needed.

Harold's first treatment was very short and he commented on this considering what it cost. Mr. Brooks replied that he would not have been able to stand anything longer at his first treatment. As we were driving home he developed a sudden runny nose and that night he had weird sensations in his head which worried us. We phoned Mr. Brooks who said that these symptoms were a good sign that the treatment was working. When the fluid had all come away the awful migraine headaches from which he had suffered ceased. They never came back so that was an immediate blessing.

The lady who had answered my first telephone enquiry, Mrs. Jean Williams, became a real friend and was a great blessing to me, in fact I feel sure I would not have kept going without her help.

**Glandular Treatment**

I went for the glandular treatment in Birmingham for several years. I had it down to a fine art – twenty minutes drive, twenty minutes treatment and twenty minutes return drive. It could all be done in Harold's lunch hour. However, when the price of petrol went up we decided to buy a machine and treat ourselves at home. It did not bring Harold's sight back but it kept us healthier for longer, until I

144

was 59, when my thyroid ceased working altogether as I shall reveal later.

## Frozen Shoulders

After some years' glandular treatment I developed a frozen shoulder. I was told that Mr. Brooks, the osteopath, could help this condition through acupuncture. The treatment took away some of the awful pain, increased the shoulder's mobility and finally released it. I did not know then that acupuncture and similar treatment from the Far East was originally linked with the occult. Friends said they thought we should not be having that sort of treatment. However, we had met many people in waiting rooms for treatment and had spread the good news of the gospel to them.

Under prompting from another friend who had once practiced acupuncture himself but had given it up, I renounced it. Harold saw no wrong in it and went on treating himself with the machine until it blew up and was unusable! The question whether to use it further no longer applied!

We went camping in August, 1978, but I was worn out, not only from packing the caravan, but also from looking after my daughter, Abi, who was very ill for two days. (Unbeknown to us, she was allergic to paint used by a decorator.) I was also in great pain from another frozen shoulder. I therefore missed some of the camp meetings. One meeting I did attend was an evening one, at which my frozen shoulder was healed. I was given a wonderful prophecy from the Lord along with the healing:

"These things that have pushed you down will no longer do so, for you will be able to walk with strength and will be able to carry these burdens and responsibilities. The strength that is now in your physical arm is also the strength of the Lord's spiritual arm. Now, as never before, a new day has come to you. You shall bear the burdens and carry the weights, knowing the secret that 'my yoke is easy and my burden is light'.[37] You have given to me, and I have given to you, for in me you have found rest. Because of the lightness in your heart, you shall understand that you do not bear the burdens alone, but I, the great burden bearer, shall walk with you in

---

[37] Matthew 11: 30

this new day. The oil of joy shall be your portion, and you will have garlands of praise in place of the spirit of heaviness."

My sister, Diana, also once had a frozen shoulder and I went with her to the hospital where she was to have it manipulated under anaesthetic. I prayed in tongues in the waiting room and told God it had been prophesied in our prayer group that an operation would not be needed. Diana was already in the hospital gown, but sensed the shoulder was free. She asked the doctor to test it before going any further. He found that it had indeed been put right as a result of prayer.

**Harold's Heart Attack**

In November 1980, my daughter, Abigail, was at boarding school in Evesham, but she came home for some weekends. During one of these she and Harold had been in the garden whilst I was working in the house. Harold came in having taken off his shirt. I had never known him do this before so I asked if he was too hot. He said he had been pulling out roses that had been planted eleven years earlier. (They were a wedding present but had become old and we had decided to get them up.) As it was now a Sunday afternoon I had prepared a meal to be eaten before I took Abi back to school. Harold started to feel pains in his chest and took some aspirin. Though he went to work next day, he made an appointment with his doctor. Four days later, after an electrocardiogram, he was told he had had a heart attack and should have a week in bed. The doctor prescribed tablets that made him drowsy and forgetful. He took these until he was cured of the need for them at a crusade meeting at Malvern in July 1981.

**Going to the Place of Death 1988-1989**

The first sign I had of a long illness was a pain in my big toe. At first I thought it was gout. My energy level started to decrease and when I woke in the morning my hands felt heavy and dead. If I carried heavy shopping my hands would become painful and sometimes they would shake. I began to put on weight and felt more and more unwell. I noticed that it became more difficult to digest certain foods that had never caused me any trouble before. I prayed about this and the Lord's answer was, "Don't go to man. Trust me. Eat foods that grow below the ground"

People began to notice the change in me and showed concern. The church house fellowship that we held at our home on Sundays and mid-week saw that I was under stress and prayed for me continually. For these prayers I shall always be thankful. I could not have carried on without them.

I had visited the doctor on another matter and told her I had just lost both my parents and that my daughter had left home. She thought my symptoms were psychological as a result of grief and stress.

My balance became very much affected and at home I hit the walls on each side of the passage that lead from our front door into the house. One day I had to go to the bank to pay the men who were doing alterations to the house. The only way I could keep reasonably straight was to say with every step I took that God is reliable, dependable, faithful, and true – a step for each word, one after the other.

My skin went pale, nearly white, and the veins stood out deep purple in contrast. My neck began to swell and I looked more bloated. My voice suddenly began to change pitch uncontrollably. When I was stressed it became shaky and stuttered. My eyes filled up with water so driving became difficult, especially at night. The pain in my big toe had spread to pains all over my body wherever there were glands. These became swollen and enlarged. My hair was falling out.

At one point I shouted to the Lord, "I can't go on like this! How can I be a good witness, looking as awful and feeling as terrible as I do?" The answer was, "Trust me. Don't go to man!" Several times I wanted to get help. If I had, I would have been given brain scans and put in a mental hospital for sure. Three friends have since said they all thought I was "going mental", and they were worried stiff. My sister had gone to a library to look up the symptoms and she had read that, if not caught in time, one could go mental. I thought I was sane. She urged me to see someone before I landed in a mental hospital.

At a dinner of the Full Gospel Business Men's Fellowship International, Dr. Calcott, whom I knew well, approached me and said, "Hello! It is Jo isn't it? I did not recognise you!" God kept his medical eyes shut for a bit longer, though I did go eventually to him for help when a packed up thyroid gland had brought me to the point of coma and in danger of death.

There was a time when the pilot light on the central heating boiler that had gone out, and I was unable to relight it, because one of the results of thyroid deficiency is thickening of the skin, like a corset. The only place where the thickening is visible is on the heels that become hardened, dry and cracked. It might have been spotted by a chiropodist but I was not attending one regularly.

One friend was also going through a long, undiagnosed, illness herself. She phoned when she felt I needed help and prayer and we used to get help for each other from the Bible.

One morning I felt so ill I did not want to make the effort to get up. The song, "Early one morning" came to mind. When I reached the words, "How could you use a poor maiden so?" I felt like saying them to God!

One of the worst symptoms was feeling extremely cold all the time and shivers of ice would go down my back. During one of these attacks I went to bed fully clothed and wearing a winter coat. The bedclothes were winter weight and I had two hot water bottles. The central heating was turned up to $74^\circ$ Fahrenheit. When my husband came home from work the heat struck him. When he found me in bed as I was, he became worried.

While I was getting supper he wandered round our dining room and found a glass statue of the Virgin and Child. My mother had originally bought the statue and given it to her sister, Eva when Eva was very ill with asthma. After my aunt died my cousin returned it to mother who kept it until her own death. Then it had been given to my daughter. Abigail did not want it so I had bought it back from her. "What's this?" Harold asked. I answered, "Oh, that's been here since Mum died." "How long have you been so ill?" he asked. I told him that it was for roughly the same time, but I had got worse from then on. We decided we would both go to God in prayer and ask to whom we should give the statue, or how we should get rid of it. The same name came to each of us, Mary Lavery. She was a Catholic lady who lived in our road and who had been a member of our house fellowship. Harold phoned and her daughter answered. Harold asked her if her mother would like to have the statue without charge as we both wanted to get rid of it. The daughter replied, "She has always wanted one of those, but will want to give you something for it." We arranged to take it. When we delivered it, both mother and daughter, Mary and Jane Lavery, were overjoyed at such a beautiful gift.

Mary Lavery took one look at me, and said, "I know what's wrong with you, because Jane went the same way." (She had recovered completely some years ago.) Mary had written to her sister, who was a doctor, and she had sent Mary a list of 25 symptoms of thyroid trouble. I had 20 of these symptoms! (Jane had had fewer.) Mary had only come upon this list just before our visit as she was clearing up. Mary told Harold to make sure I went to the doctor's the next morning. I did, and I asked for a thyroid test to be done. The results came through on Harold's birthday, February 27th. The doctor was amazed that my count was only 3, way below the normal point of coma and death which was 12. He told me I needed to take Thyroxin straight away and to continue to take them for the rest of my life. I replied that God had told me he was going to take me through the "valley of the shadow" and the way of sacrifice. I wanted to find out if God wanted to heal me by a miracle or by taking the tablets. (I wanted prayer and help from Dr. Calcott first.) My doctor told me not to leave it too long or I might be dead. I said I had nearly died several times before, and only by the grace of God was I alive.

I phoned Dr. Calcott who had been away. He said that God had told him to return home sooner than planned as someone was in need of his help. This person was at the point of death. He said, "Come over straight away." I felt so ill I wondered if I was safe to drive, or should I ask someone to take me? The Lord said, "Go, and I will be with you."

That day, March 1st, all manner of things went wrong in the house. I took 20 minutes to lay the table; my brain was so slowed down. I could not get a handful of cutlery from the drawer and slap them on the table. I had to count each item for each person. I burnt the toast badly and the room filled with smoke. Then a cup on the draining board fell over by itself. I felt that the "Old D." was present and that he was angry that he was going to be dealt with.

When I arrived at Dr. Douglas Calcott's, he and his wife Elizabeth were there. I was in my thickest winter clothes. They had a roaring gas fire and were feeling far too hot but, for my sake, they suffered the heat a little longer. They had a special way of working that they called "Praise, Promise and Problem" (the three "Ps"). Their method was allow time for people to relax and then commit all to the Lord. They ask God for cleansing, then think of the question, but concentrate on praising the Saviour and remembering his promises. The problem is lastly brought before the Lord and silence is kept for his reply. This may take the form of a mental picture, a story, or a scripture reference.

They put, as the problem; did God want to heal me by a miracle or by the Thyroxin? We prayed and offered praise, then kept silence, waiting for an answer and a promise. Elizabeth had a vision of an altar with a white sheet upon it and a sacrificial lamb. Douglas saw the bitter water of Mara being made sweet. I saw Isaac on the pyre, waiting for Abraham to kill him with a knife but stopped from doing so by God who supplied a ram caught in a thicket. [38]They explained that the tablets are made from a lamb. This seemed to mean that I was to take the Thyroxin, but at the same time pray for healing and also the healing of family relationships that had put such a strain on me and caused my thyroid to go wrong in the first place.

I went back to my doctor and said I would take the tablets. He asked me how I had arrived at that decision. I told him all that had taken place at Dr. Calcott's home; a witness to give God all the glory.

I have just read a book entitled "The Heavenly Man" by Brother Yun and Paul Hattaway.[39] The description of years of dreadful suffering in Chinese prisons makes my suffering hardly worth mentioning, but it seemed bad enough to me, though I felt closer to God through it than I did in the good times. Since then there have been other ways He has taught me to trust Him rather than humans or my own ability and reasoning.

**Diabetes**

The first sign of diabetes for Harold was when he had had an argument with his brother over the simple matter of a gift. Next day his doctor discovered Harold's blood sugar level was 24 when a level of 5 is considered normal. So a diet without sugar was

---

[38] Genesis 22:12
[39] Monarch Books, paperback, 2002

prescribed. This continued for many years before the doctor said that diet control and tablets were no longer sufficient. He would have to put him onto insulin injections. Harold dreaded having to face needles, since he had had a terrible year of lumbar punctures as a child. I knew how he felt, and that I would have to learn how to inject, so we both wanted to delay matters. Fear is of the devil, but I feared I would do it wrongly and perhaps kill him; or that I might give the wrong dosage, or forget to do it, or cause an infection, or a hundred and one other things. I knew, for example, that it was dangerous if an air bubble was in the insulin pen.

These fears affected me badly. I recalled sitting next my Father as a child asking for help with my homework. The method of arithmetic he had been taught was different from the method I had been taught, so I was confused and said I could not do my sums. He said that of course I could, otherwise I would never be any good. Faced with having to inject Harold, some 50 years later, these feelings returned and I wrote the following poem to relieve them:

Old age is seen in these trembling hands,
The mind is forgetful of all its plans,
Stress is shown by the lack of peace,
Only through prayer can I find release.

Working things out can take me back
To when my Father showed up my lack
Of knowledge of sums – so hard for me,
Yet to him the answers came easily.

"Don't put back your ears; don't resist being shown
How to do schoolwork you should have known."
These were his words as I sped away.
Yet still I returned at a later day.

My tears are now beginning to flow,
Though I hid them then, as I feared to show
Just how I was feeling, outwardly,
When accused by him of stupidity.

Yet now I think, from my earliest days,
Trouble bore fruit in different ways.

I learned, from the greatest difficulty,
To be what the Lord intended for me.

A letter arrived from the hospital asking us to see a specialist who would show us how to use a pen of insulin, take a blood sample, read and note the result. Since we had a special dispensation for our age and for Harold's blindness, we can use our surgery for prescriptions. The nurse at the surgery used a different make of equipment from that at the hospital. However, she gave me a demonstration, and wrote down on paper the procedure for each item. There was also a daunting booklet of 56 pages on the use of blood test equipment! I learnt by heart the equivalent of an A4 page of instructions, and my daily scripture readings were a great help at this time. I was to "put on the whole armour of God"[40] against the panic attacks of the devil. The first time we did a test was the 16th November 2004. It took 20 minutes to accomplish, though two years later we were able to do it in 5 minutes. The days are fewer when the message "Error 4" or "Error 5" comes up on the screen. Harold is one of the few people from whom it is difficult to draw blood. One experienced nurse had to take a sample from the back of his hand, having already tried several times in both arms without getting a drop. Harold objects to more than one prick, so I have to pinch and squeeze him to obtain a large enough blood droplet for the test to register. We gain wisdom when we wrestle with difficulties. Insulin injections must be done at the same time each day if possible. We had to discipline ourselves to rise at 7.30 a.m. instead of getting up when we felt like doing so. So through regular check-ups Harold's diabetes has been controlled, though this has sometimes meant changing the brand of drugs used.
In my family there were no cases of diabetes, and I myself loved sweet things. I ate the icing from cakes so Harold did not have the sugary part. I also loved treacle, jams, marmalade, honey and so forth. However, it was a great shock to me to discover, the day before we set off in our caravan, that my own blood sugar level was high. I had to unpack all the sugary foods I had already put in the van!

---

[40] See foot note 26

The first shared tea at the camp seemed to have everything I now should not eat. "Lord, lead us not into temptation," I said. I also asked why God had allowed me to have diabetes. The answer came, "You need self-discipline." I had, indeed, been pleasing myself in many things, especially sweet ones, but I had no idea that sugar had made me so heavy! Things might have been worse had I not taken the dog, Uska, out for walks every day. Working in the garden had also helped burn off excess sugar. In the next three weeks I lost a stone and another stone over the next three months. At nine and a half stone, my face and neck show wrinkles, so when people say, "You've lost weight" they are probably thinking I look old.

Fortunately, like my Father, I hoard things. Although many clothes no longer fit me, I was able to find some from the years when I was slimmer that do fit. I do not want the complications that come with diabetes, so I am strict with myself. I eat raisins or dates instead of confectionary, and use sugar substitutes in a cake from which I take no more than one slice a day as a treat.

**Dementia**

My husband has suffered a form of dementia, partly due to his diabetes and partly due to damage to his brain from childhood Tubercular Meningitis. We are grateful that we have been undergirded by the prayers of hundreds of people. We are also grateful to God for his answers so that we have been able to keep active and enjoy life. One of the advantages of frequent visits to hospitals is that we have opportunities to witness to others what God has done for us. When I talk with specialists I always tell them that in addition to taking drugs for healing or keeping the illnesses under control, prayer is also being offered up.

**An unknown condition**

At the age of 77, the day before the 43$^{rd}$ anniversary of when I was born again, I went for one of the annual health check-ups that I call MOTs (after the compulsory Ministry of Transport tests for motor vehicles over 3 years old). To start with, the nurse could not find a vein from which to take blood. She tried 3 times in different places and got nothing. I said aloud, "Please, Jesus, help me" and next try the blood poured out. A booking was made for me to go back for the results two weeks later. The results showed cholesterol was 2 and sugar normal, kidney and liver alright and blood pressure slightly high but not high enough for treatment. I had lost some weight and there had been a change in bowel function so the doctor asked me to return so that she could have a look inside my bowel. I asked for prayer support from friends and family. I entered the surgery for the examination with praise on my lips. The doctor wanted to refer me to a specialist for my peace of mind. I told her I had peace of mind because in the 1970s an endocrinologist had said that I would have lumps or growths, but they would be non-cancerous. I had taken him at his word and not been for the breast or cervical screening that one could ask for as a precautionary measure if one were over the age of 65. Nevertheless, the doctor asked for an appointment and thought I might get one within a couple of weeks because the changes had started two months previously. As I left the surgery the nurse said "Take someone with you." The Easter holiday intervened, but the appointment was made.

I therefore phoned the hospital appointments secretary to ask if I would need a driver or could I go alone? She said if it was my first visit it would be a clinic and I would not receive treatment then.

I think we all fear the unknown. I had early experienced this fear when doctors stood round my bed when I was four years old and my ears were pierced to save mastoids. I was also fearful when about to give birth to my daughter, Abigail. This time there was more prayer support and uplifting words. While waiting I prayed, "Lord, why this trouble when you know how much my husband needs me to be on hand to help him with his insulin injections, with the 14 tablets he takes, with his mobility, his blindness and his dementia?" The answer was, "Are you struggling to see God's purpose in your suffering today? You can rest assured that he has one." I wondered what that purpose was, and my daily readings said it was "to grow in maturity, to strengthen trust, and develop character; to be used to show God's glory and his provision in times of need, and to bring God into everything." He had all my affairs in his hands. Through Maundy Thursday and Good Friday I realised again how Jesus faced his problem of crucifixion. What was my little bit of a problem compared with that? Because we often had broken nights, since the guide dog would wake us to be let out or to have his breakfast, I would spend the time reading if I did not sleep afterwards. The Bible is a great help in difficult times, for example when the

154

disciples were terrified in a storm, [41] Jesus said, "Why are you so afraid? Do you still have no faith?"

Another source of help was the Carers' Group that had its first meeting in our church hall. Also several people at I talked with at church had been through similar experiences to mine. They said I should not go alone to see the specialist. However, I could not ask busy people who are at work, and I could not think of anyone else. So I decided against attempting to control and organise things. If motivated by self will rather than trust in God I would regret it. God's Holy Spirit would show me his plans for me that would be accomplished. I thought, "Thanks, Lord, I know you will keep me waiting until the last minute before you show me the person you want to accompany me to see the specialist."

Shortly afterward I took my husband to the surgery for a diabetes injection, and the nurse who did it enquired of me how I had got on with the doctor. I told her I was to see a specialist and she said, "Take someone with you". I replied, "I already have Jesus with me, and I don't mind waiting because I can pray for the other people in the waiting area."

Nevertheless I took note because there is a saying that we should heed what comes from the mouths of two witnesses. So I was not surprised when at church, during the exchanging of the "Peace", a friend said, "Would you like me to accompany you to the specialist?" This lady was a nurse and therefore knew what might be done. After looking inside me, the specialist asked if I had any heart trouble or pains. I said I had none. They then wanted to take a scan, as they thought from feeling me I might have an aneurism. The scan was made and, praise God, there was only a thickened artery. I did have further treatment consisting of complete cleansing of the system from stomach to anus, with pictures of everything. There was nothing to worry about. I used to eat uncooked mixture when baking cakes, so it might have been salmonella from raw egg. I have given up the habit and remained healthy since.

---

[41] Mark 4: 40-41

## CHAPTER THIRTEEN: DEATHS IN THE FAMILY
### Harold's Father

The first of our parents to die was Harold's Father, Reginald Bagby, known as Reg. He and Harold's mother had moved to a council flat in order to be nearer to us for their later years. These years were shorter than we thought. We came back from a camping holiday in July to find a note from Harold's brother saying their Dad was in hospital and had undergone various tests. The doctors thought he had a hiatus hernia. He had also had a prostate operation and was not at all well. He got worse. He was unable to swallow or keep food down. One day he said, "I've got cancer of the stomach". He knew the symptoms as one of his friends had died of it not long before. Doctors kept saying it was hiatus hernia. One afternoon I called in and was horrified at how he looked. He showed me what he had vomited into a bucket, not food, but pints of a horrible greenish-yellow mess. I phoned his doctor and said, "I don't think you are doing enough for my father-in-law. Will you visit him, for he's in a bad way?" Next day I heard he had been taken back into hospital for further tests and investigations.

Harold and I prayed much for him and one day while I was praying, God gave me the following message: "I will take him to the point of death. He will see me and live." I told Harold, and we both wondered if "live" meant a miracle healing or life in the world to come after death.

In early October we were called to see him as they were going to operate. They found a huge cancer that could have been dealt with in July for it was in an operable area. He came through, but then caught pneumonia as he was by then very weak and just skin and bones. We were told to gather the rest of the family to say our "Goodbyes". Other members went in first and then Harold and I on our own. He was in intensive care, on a ventilator, with nine tubes in and out of his body. The nurse left us with him and we said "The Lord's Prayer" as our friends Alec and Mary Learmont had taught us. "Our Father (in Reg), hallowed be Thy name (in Reg), Thy kingdom come (in Reg), Thy will be done (in Reg), on earth". The nurse then came rushing in saying, "Whatever you are doing, please, will you stop it. I have never seen the machinery go so haywire in my life!" We told her that we only said "The Lord's Prayer" over him. We looked at Dad and he raised his left eyebrow (he was too weak to do anything else) to let us know he had met Jesus and given his life to him. We went home to get lunch for the rest of the family and the phone rang to say he had passed to glory. We had many times tried to lead him to Jesus, but, like the thief on the cross, he was saved at the last moment. Of this we have no doubt at all.

We had the funeral from our home as we could accommodate all the family for refreshments afterwards. My sister and sister-in-law helped. Reg Senior was cremated and the ashes buried at Beoley church which Harold's brother and his wife attended.

Reg. Junior asked his mother, in my hearing, "Well, Mum, you see what we have done for Dad, would you like the same done for you when your time comes?" She replied, "Yes, please." Little did anyone know we would be dealing with her funeral only 6 weeks after that of Dad.

**Harold's Mother**

Harold's mother was a diabetic and had been kept to a strict diet and to a regime of tablets when Dad was alive. Somehow things went badly wrong. She asked me what the cause of a black tongue was. She then stuck hers out to show me it was black. Next day the warden on her rounds found Mum sick in bed and called the doctor. She phoned me to say the doctor had sent her to Birmingham General Hospital.

We went to visit her in the early afternoon of a Sunday. We left Abigail with the vicar and his children, at the invitation of the vicar's wife. At the hospital we met other relations, and Mum seemed quite cheerful and talked to us. However, we did not stay long as there were so many visitors wanting to see her. Later the hospital phoned to say there had been a serious deterioration in her condition and they did not think she would last the night, and could the family come. Harold was at work and phoned his brothers at their work and all reached the hospital around 4.30 p.m. I stayed home with Abigail as we had an evening Bible Study meeting at home, to be led by the minister. The meeting was just starting when Harold phoned to say she had gone to be with Jesus, and we knew she had given her life to Him. She actually died in Harold's arms with the rest gathered round. We held the funeral at our house as before.

Abigail was 9 years old at the time, and said she would like to go to the funeral parlour. I wondered if she was too young, but I felt Jesus would be with us to help her. It was a short while after Gran's ashes were buried next to Granddad's that I found Abi crying and asked her what was the matter. She said she was crying for Gran. Without thinking, I said, "She's fine in heaven with Jesus and Granddad." These words had such an effect on her that she could not cry later when my parents died. (She did later thank me for making her strong and able to control her tears when she had to face divorce after 10 years of marriage.)

## Harold's youngest brother, Peter

The next death was that of Harold's 22-year-old brother, Peter Bagby. He was involved in a motorcar accident while abroad on holiday. We were in Malvern at the time at a "Good News Crusade" camp. Harold's sister and her husband came to tell us that Peter had died after a car, driven by one of his friends, had hit a tree. (No other vehicle was involved.) The group of friends had been drinking, but would not let Peter drive. Peter was in a back seat, and was apparently winded. When he had stopped breathing they gave over-vigorous heart massage, which made his condition worse, and he died. There had to be an inquest in Norway so we had to wait 2 weeks for the funeral. All Peter's motor cyclist friends gave the funeral procession in Birmingham a guided pathway through the traffic. The undertakers allowed the family to see Peter's face inside the coffin. It was not a pretty sight. I saw it for Harold's sake but did not let Abigail look.

It seems Peter had stayed previously with these friends and, while there, had had a very vivid dream that frightened him so much he told Harold about it. In the dream he saw his father (who had died beforehand). His father was trying to get Peter to go with him somewhere. Harold told Peter the dream was a warning from Dad not to go back to stay with those friends again. He did go, and lost his life.

## Harold's older brother, Reginald

Reginald died after falling down a flight of stairs. His injuries caused his brain to swell, and though the hospital did all they could to save his life, he died four days later, in spite of much prayer being offered up for him.

## My Father

My father, John Pheysey had a stroke in October 1985 and was ill in hospital for a time but was determined to become mobile enough to be home for my mother's birthday on 31$^{st}$ October. He managed this, and, with determination he improved, though he dragged one leg and needed a Zimmer frame. It was St. Peter's Day, June 29$^{th}$ 1986, when he had another more severe stroke at home. Mother heard him shout and found him on the toilet seat where she had to prop him up until my sister returned from an early morning service at church. They called an ambulance and he was taken to hospital in Kidderminster. My sister knew we had a Sunday morning house group so she phoned us at lunch time to say that if we wanted to see him alive we had better come over as he would not last long.

Harold and I sat in prayer together and Harold had a vision of a stage with curtains coming down at the end of a show. So we knew it was to be the end of his life, but wondered what he looked like and whether to take our daughter. I phoned the hospital and was told he was not disfigured but a little blue in the hands and face. The nurse we contacted by phone was a Christian and I had told her that we were. She said he was very ill and I saw a black cross while on the phone. She said not to delay.

Abigail decided she would prefer not to go, so we left her with friends. She thought Granddad would not like her to see him in the state he was in. So she went to friends who prayed with us before we left. Before we returned to collect her we phoned to tell her he had died.

On the way to Kidderminster Hospital I remembered how Jesus, as he was dying, handed his mother over to his disciple, John. I felt Dad was handing Mum over to Harold as the only male in the near circle.

It was a boiling hot day so we asked God for shade in which to park, for the guide dog's sake, as he had to be left in the car. There was no shady place but God sent clouds over the sun for the whole time we were inside the hospital. (The sun came out again the minute we returned to the car!)

When we arrived I said, "Hello, Dad, it is Jo here." He then drew my hand to his chest through the bars round the bed. The Christian nurse came in to remove his false teeth and said prayer was the best help he could have. After she left I prayed for him to have peace and rest. I told him he had fought the good fight and could let go and be with Jesus who would never fail nor forsake him. He moved his hand to show he understood. Then we sang hymns to him. I held his hand, and, to let us know that he heard us, he moved his first finger up and down to the beat of the hymn or song. Harold said, "He's the last sheaf of wheat left in a cornfield, waiting to be gathered in." Several times he stopped breathing and I went for a nurse who said he would do this before dying. My sister returned with Mother and we said our "Good Byes". We agreed we would take the dog for a walk and meet later at my parents' home for a meal. When we were in the car Harold said, "Before we sit down to a meal there will be a phone call to say he's gone". Later we were all at the table, about to say grace, when the phone rang to say he had gone to be with Jesus. The same nurse to whom I had spoken on the previous telephone call told us next morning when I collected the death certificate that she was with him when he died. She said he had just stopped breathing. There was no struggle, fight, or choking and a look of peace came over him. There was no waxy look of death at all.

We knew he had given his life to Jesus at a house meeting of friends some years before.

At the undertakers we saw his body. It was laid out, dressed in white robes and with his hands folded on his chest. Mother said, "Oh, doesn't he look like a bishop!" Dad was a farmer and normally wore farmer's clothes. Mum then said, "You sang to him in the hospital didn't you?" So we sang a few choruses, beginning with "We are one in spirit, we are one in the Lord." Harold saw a light shining onto Father. He asked if there was a sunlit window. There was none, but the person in charge said there had formerly been one there. We realised that the light Harold saw was Dad's spiritual cord. It was being cut to free him from his body. God has a sense of humour, for what came to my mind was "Now t'worms will come and eat thee up" from "Ilkley Moor Bar T'at".

The following day God answered more of my prayers. He made the way for all that had to be done straight and clear. The undertaker had helpfully explained everything that was necessary, so I was not flustered, and the lady at the Registry Office said it was unusual for so few people to be there. I told her it was God's plan to make things easy for me. He even sent shade for Mum to sit in the car while I went to register the death.

Later, with God's help, I found a printer who would print the memorial service and a flower shop for family flowers. Abigail wanted to wear a hat but did not have one. We found one in time.

It was 7 hours between Dad's final stroke and his death, 3 days before we saw his body at the undertakers, and 7 days from his death until the burial of his ashes in Broome churchyard in the family grave where his parents' bodies lay. Again, God's 3 and 7 numbers! The coffin was moved to Broome church where it lay over the Thursday night after he died, then, on the Friday, there was a service at the crematorium for family only. The memorial service later, in Broome Church, was relayed to the Church Hall, as the church could not accommodate all who wanted to come. A family friend paid tribute to him during the service, and I made a scrapbook of Dad's life for people to look at while refreshments were served in the Hall.

## My Mother

After Dad's death Diana took our mother, Dorothy Pheysey from our parents' home to her own bungalow where she cared for her, for by then Mother had had a stroke herself and used a wheel chair. She made the effort to come to us on the first Christmas after Dad died because she wanted us to have happy Christmas memories by which to remember her.

The following Christmas she asked my sister what present she would like and the reply was, "A little longer in bed on Christmas morning." When the day came, mother woke early as was her wont, and my sister thought she had forgotten. They had a proper Christmas lunch together and then my sister tucked Mum back in bed for her afternoon rest. "Just rest until I wake you", she said. She wanted to take a present to another old lady who was alone on Christmas day. Imagine her surprise when she returned to find an empty bed where Mum should have been. She went into the kitchen and found the dirty lunch dishes washed and stacked in the rack and the table set for breakfast. Mum was in her chair in the lounge, completely exhausted. Instead of being grateful my sister scolded her. "How ever did you manage to do that?" she asked. "God gave me strength", Mum answered.

On the day of the Epiphany, 6<sup>th</sup> January, my sister had a long-standing and very important task to fulfil, a long distance away. Mum was too poorly to be left and, on January 5<sup>th</sup>, I was asked to stay with her. I made arrangements for Abigail to look after her father, put a few things in a suitcase, and set off. While driving to my sister's I heard very clearly God speaking to me, "Though I take thee through the valley of the shadow of death, I will be with thee." Mum was in bed when I arrived on the 5<sup>th</sup>, and I discovered she had had a stroke at 11.15 p.m. the same time that I had felt ill myself. A similar coincidence had happened before. When she saw me Mum asked if I had come to stay with her. I replied, "Yes, for as long as you need me." She asked me, weakly, if I would open the window when she settled. I stayed with her that night and the next day. I was wondering how I could cope alone, when friends called and one of them offered to stay with me. This friend had seen people die and was telling me what she knew, which helped me to be prepared for Mum's passing. The doctor and health visitor called to organise help and equipment. My sister returned and took over that night. I had "the shakes" and thought it was food poisoning and went to the kitchen for bicarbonate of soda. My sister was in the kitchen and asked what I wanted. As I replied my voice changed pitch uncontrollably and she gave me a drink and I returned to bed. In the morning my sister phoned the doctor about me and he said there was a bug going around and I should stay in bed. My sister looked after us and let in the many callers who came to say "Good bye" to Mum. They came to see me too.

During the following night I had an encounter with the "Enemy", and also with God. I was praying for Mum to have an easy passage because she had once been involved with the occult. This could have made difficulties for her. I was reading my Bible and I was struck by the words, "Get rid of the idols and purify yourselves". [42]

I knew what the idols were – some wooden figures once carved for Mum – and asked my sister to get rid of them, as it was very important they were out of the house. They were put in a disused poultry shed.

---

[42] Genesis 35: 2

A cousin Bill and his wife called to pray with and for me before they went to work. Remembering my promise to be with Mum for as long as she needed me, I prayed that if I went in to her my voice would sound natural again. I did go in and said, "I'm still here, Mum."

Early in the morning of 10th January my sister called the doctor in, and I joined them. Mother was struggling to get her breath, and he gave her an injection. I think Mum was wondering "How long?" because I remembered she had told me she had said those words to a doctor during labour when my sister was born. We asked, "How long?" He replied, "Probably today". We showed him out and returned to Mum. She was half propped up in bed, and, as we entered, she opened her eyes wide as if she had seen someone, and then fell back on the pillows. We thought she may have seen Dad waiting for her. My sister went out to make breakfast and I held Mum's hand. She suddenly gripped me with such strength that I said, "Mum, what a grip!" She did it again firmly, and then she was gone. I said, "Father into your hands I commend her spirit. Jesus is Lord over all." I went and told my sister and she brought a mirror to see if there was any moisture on it from breath. She said, "I think you're right." She gave me a hug and I said, "It's what we prayed for, a peaceful passing."

We had breakfast together and afterwards I phoned Harold and Abigail before they left for work or college. Abigail answered and said she had been awake during the night, worrying about me. I told her I would be home by night time, though my sister had invited me to stay with her if I wished. Harold said, "The time she died she skipped and gambolled through the room I was in, and I knew she was free of her body and on the way to heaven!"

I prayed to the Lord, asking whom Mum had seen before she died. The tune came to mind of "Mine eyes have seen the glory of the coming of the Lord."[43] I asked the Lord if she had seen him, why hadn't I seen him. He replied that what she saw was "Me in you". So He had used my body to reveal Himself to her as we stood in the doorway. This was a wonderful revelation, and I praised and thanked Jesus for it.

---

[43] Battle Hymn of the Republic, Julia Ward Howe, 1819-1910

The doctor came back just 45 minutes after his previous visit to confirm her passing, and agreed with me that she had been inwardly asking, "How long?" It was a shorter time than the doctor had predicted, so thank God he knew how much she could take. (This is in His Word.)[44] I heard the hymn, "Through the night of doubt and sorrow, onward goes the pilgrim band, singing songs of expectation, marching to the Promised Land."[45] So I knew Mum was, indeed, on the way to the Promised Land.

The nurse who came to collect the aids and equipment praised my sister for the way she had looked after Mother. She had met Mum's needs in the physical realm for over 8 years.

The undertaker was a Christian. I had met him before at a Full Gospel dinner. He shared with me his readings for the day. They spoke of Mum's wonderful nature and beliefs.

Mum had left us an example of courage and endurance and spirit. She also left letters for us to read after her death, which we read while awaiting the undertaker. Her letter to me spoke of the difference in her faith after she became a committed Christian, and how she wished she had been one when I was searching for a faith and explored Spiritualism. She could have helped me more at that time of my life.

I got home to find Harold already there on compassionate leave. I phoned Abigail to let her know I was home again and then I went to bed. When Abi came home she came into the bedroom and sat on the bed holding my hand to comfort me. She was also tired. She then went to her room to read the letter Mum had left for her.

Mum had left her body to Birmingham medical School but we were able to see it at the undertakers first. We were glad to sing choruses, one of which was, "I see in you the glory of my King and we love you in the love of the Lord." Mum's face had a thin, faint, smile and a look of peace, unlike the stressed look from the illness. We had a memorial service later and I kept letters of condolence and noted how they all said what a wonderful lady she was.

---

[44] 1 Corinthians 10: 13

[45] Bernhardt Ingleman, tr. Sabine Baring-Gould (1834-1924) in Ancient and Modern Revised

Before she died she had told me she did not want us to grieve or wear black, for she would be glad to go. I wondered what to wear. I had recently given Abigail £100 for clothes to wear at an interview. God said, "I want you to do the same for yourself." I asked, "Where do I go? What do I get? Who will go with me?" A verse about being jewels in His crown came to my mind, so I thought, "The dress must be like a lot of splendid jewels!" I did not have enough faith to withdraw the money from my account, but went to the cheaper shops. They had nothing remotely like jewels. Finally, I went to *Marks and Spencer* and saw the very dress, but it was not my size. Then I was reminded that I had not obeyed God and withdrawn the cash. I went through the shop to the door, and there, beside the door, on the front of a rack of men's clothes was the dress I wanted and in my size for £27. I took it to the till and asked if they would keep it until I came back from the bank with the money. Then I thought about getting a coat to match one of the many splendid jewel colours. *British Home Stores* had a red three-quarter red one, but not in my size. I went to *Owen and Owen* and they had a one, a perfect match to the blue in the dress, in the right size with a sale price of £55. I already had a suitable hat, bag, and shoes, but Abigail had said I must smarten myself up for the new clothes by getting my hair done. So, when I was passing a unisex hairdresser, I asked if they could do my hair without an appointment. They could, so I had my hair cut and set. On the day of the thanksgiving service for Mum's life, I felt it was quite in order not to wear black in view of Mum's request. It also gave me a chance to witness how I came to buy the clothes.

**CHAPTER FOURTEEN: GOD'S PROVISION AND PROTECTION**

**How God provided for our house extension**

God started speaking to us in 1970 about enlarging the house at the rear, next to the kitchen, where there was an open veranda from which five steps dropped down into the garden. A glass roof and doors to convert part of the veranda would cost £750 which was a lot in those days. We would have liked a larger extension but could not afford it. What we planned would serve a number of uses – play room for Abigail, dining area (currently part of the lounge) or more space for the kitchen. We invited a builder whom we had used before. Construction started in July and ended in September, and we were more than pleased with the results. It got very warm in the summer and helped to keep out cold winds in the winter. We had it blessed as we had done with the rest of the house and we thanked God for it.

We wanted the new logia to continue from outside the kitchen so that it ran along outside the lounge also. We could not afford this. However, once more, we were given the instruction to enlarge our borders, so we prayed for the finance needed. God had, as usual, prepared the way long before we discovered it. I had been the beneficiary of a Trust set up by my father that involved my sister, Diana, also and the cousin who took over the farm later when Father had retired. For several years family members did the Trust accounts. When they could no longer continue to do this, they handed the accounts to a professional accountant. He asked me to give him details of what I had received over twenty years. I had kept every statement and cheque stubs from my twenty-first birthday onwards, and I was then over fifty, so this was no problem. When the accountant compared what I had received with what I should have been paid he discovered that the Trust owed me £10,000. This paid for the logia extension for which we were hoping and praying.

We had a gathering of family and friends for a meal there and a blessing ceremony in January 1983. It has been a great blessing since sliding doors allow its use as an extension to the lounge, so we have extra room for prayer meetings and church groups as well as for celebratory occasions. The people who did the work were

Christians who lived in the next village and held meetings that we attended in their homes. They did a very good job in making new foundations, whereas the earlier work outside the kitchen had been placed on a veranda.

In 1986 my father died and we used his legacy to convert our garage into a dining room. It was beyond the bathroom, so we also had space for a small shower cubicle. By this time we had a bigger car with a tow bar for a caravan and the garage was too small. However, when we had bought the house the previous owner said that the garage would be easily convertible as it had been built with double bricks. God was preparing the way for later developments.

Several times the builder asked for interim payments at moments when I was busy serving our evening meal, and I did not have time to check everything before I paid. However, the Holy Spirit made me aware that something had been done wrongly, so I was able to put things right rather than start legal action. We should pray over everything we decide to do, seeking if it is God's will before we go ahead.

**God showed me the way and met my need**

On one occasion I was lost in Cheshire, when I was going to see a friend who had moved there. I stopped to ask a lady the way and she said, "I live next door to your friend. I've finished my shopping and was just going to catch a bus back, but now you can take me and I can show you the way." Out of all the people whom I could have asked, I asked that lady! Who says we have not got a helping angel?

God knows our needs and can get an answer to us quickly. A demonstration of this was when I was single and was wondering how to get to a shop to buy stamps and post letters that needed to go that day. The car petrol was very low and I was also booked to visit a sick person some distance away, but I had no money. My sister was out and there was no one else in the house except for a great uncle, whom she was looking after. No sooner had I asked God for help, than he shouted out, "Jo! Come here a minute." I went to my sister's dining room where he was sitting at the table holding a pound note in his hand. He said, "I know you are looking after me this weekend as your sister is away. Here's a pound to get food." I went to the nearest garage to get petrol, to the shops for food and for stamps, posted the letters and then drove on to see the little boy, Mark, who was too poorly to come to me. (You would not be able to do all that for a pound today.) God did the work of influencing our great uncle to give me the money. I later repaid what I had used for my own items, though not the food he wanted, and told my great uncle how God had used him to answer my arrow prayer.

## Protection from injury

A dramatic instance of God's protection was when I was lifting an old wrought-iron bedstead up into the roof loft above our hall. I was using a step ladder that hardly reached the loft opening. When I was up to the top step, with the bed above my head half-way into the loft, the steps spread-eagled and went flat to the floor. I hung onto the bed frame which landed level on the floor and then fell away to the door-post of a nearby room. I landed upright with no bones broken and not even a bruise. A rug in the hall had wrapped itself round a nearby pillar. My great uncle, who was in the house at the time, shouted, "What on earth has happened?" I said, "I've only come from loft to floor in one fell swoop with a bedstead." The shock came out next day, but I was fine otherwise.

Another time I was going down the stairs in my mother's house with a vacuum. I caught my heel in a skirt hem that, unbeknown to me, had come unstitched. I was caught off balance and could have gone down the stairs, which were long and steep, on my back, but God's hand caught me.

## Protection in fog

One November I was invited to Ollerton, a village near Worksop, to take an evening service of Divine Healing at the church there, and to stay for the night afterwards at the home of my friend Mike Hall. Having seen on the map that Ollerton was near Worksop, I wrote to another friend, the Rev. Neil asking if I could see him in the afternoon on my way. He gave me tea and then we saw fog descending, so I left early. The fog got worse and worse. As I had no knowledge of the roads I needed to see the sign posts. I was on my own but not alone. I somehow reached Ollerton, and then sent a prayer for help. "Do I stop or go on, or what do I do?" I saw a light at a butcher's shop. It had a half open stable door type of entrance. That is why the light was visible. I went in and asked the way. The butcher said, "It's difficult enough to find your way in daylight let alone fog. There is a housing estate of many roads." So I sat in the car and prayed, "Lord, you have got me this far. Now what do you want me to do?" Then there was a tap on the car window. It was Mike, who said that God had told him that I was in the vicinity and that he was to go out and look for me. He said if I had been anywhere else he would not have known whether to go to the left or the right. He got into the driver's seat and we drove to his house for a meal. We then had to drive to the church which was some distance away. We passed over a main road to a dual carriage way. I had my window down, trying to see the road to help Mike. I said, "Watch out, I can hear a heavy vehicle coming down the road towards us. Pull over." An accident was avoided!

I did not expect anyone to turn up at the church but a good number had made the effort, as everyone thought others would not go. After the service we were invited round to the Vicarage for tea and coffee and biscuits and to chat further on the subject of healing.

It was very late when we got back to Mike's and to bed. With all that had gone on I had a job to get to sleep. I felt cold and soon started to feel sick. I had sickness all night and I said to Mike at breakfast, "Pray for me or I will need a bowl and a chamber pot to drive over 100 miles home." He prayed and I did not need either until I was home. I then needed both immediately!

I had time to rest and sleep before turning out in the afternoon to speak to a Mothers Union meeting and again in the evening for a meeting of The Guild of Health in Birmingham. I had promised to take other people to this and one of them received healing for her ankle. Praise the Lord for healing me and strengthening me for that day's tasks! Before I knew Jesus I had regular bilious attacks that would last all night and keep me in bed the next day. I would feel weak for days afterwards and my chest would be painful from heaving up bile.

## CHAPTER FIFTEEN: CELEBRATIONS
### Meetings with Her Majesty the Queen

In the "Year of the Disabled", we were invited to a Buckingham Palace Garden Party. One of the ladies I had helped had been a dressmaker, and her way of saying thank you was to make me a dress to wear for the Garden Party. We were taken there by a kind friend, Arthur Newbold, who was determined to get us right up to the palace steps and explained, when stopped by police, that he had a blind man and his dog as passengers.

This was my second visit as my father had received the Order of the British Empire in 1967. On that occasion we decided to have tea in one of the huge tea tents. We heard a commotion and people leaving, but by the time we got out, the crowd were twenty deep, so we only saw the top of her hat. This time, in order to get a better view, we decided not to take tea until after the Queen had appeared. There were still about five rows of people in front. The dog, Honey, was upset, as all she could see were legs. She whined just as an usher was passing. He said, "What's going on here? Oh it's a dog and it's got claustrophobia, poor thing. Will you make way for them to come to the front, please?" The crowds parted like the Red Sea. So Harold and Honey went to the front. The usher then asked, "Who has accompanied him?" I put up my hand and he again asked the crowd to part for me. He asked for some information about Harold, where he was from, his job and so on, and off he went to tell the Queen and escort her to us. I wondered if I should take Harold's arm and push it forward for her to shake, but she was already taking hold of his hand whilst I did a curtsey. They talked about switchboards in the Palace and in the Council House. Harold said to her, "You must come to see our New Town Hall building. Only the footings have been laid so far." (Years later she did come to open the Town Hall, and Harold was in the line of people waiting to meet her. She walked up to him and said, "I do like your New Town Hall". She had remembered him from the garden party.)

We went for tea after the Queen had left and enjoyed it very much. At the appointed departure time our taxi was at the door to collect us. We had a pleasant journey home. (Dear Mr. Newbold, our driver, died only a short while ago.)

Years before then, my husband, Harold, was awarded the British Empire Medal for his services to the community as a telephonist at Redditch Borough Council. Harold received his actual medal on June 17th 1985, at the hands of the Queen's representative, the Lord Lieutenant of the County at a party at Redditch Town Hall. The Queen had written saying she was sorry she could not present the award herself.

## My 60th Birthday

Having recovered from a long illness, I wanted to share with relations and friends the joy of being given my life back again, and to give God the glory. Walkwood Community Centre Hall, which was only two and a half miles from here, was free for the date of my party.

My daughter, Abi, was by then working in the hotel industry and knew a lady who did food for parties. I arranged with her what to have, and for how many. I said I would make the large cakes as my contribution. I was wondering how to transport the cakes I had made safely in the car, and thought a baker's bread tray would be ideal to stop them sliding off the seat. (This mishap had happened to me years before when I was going to a WI cookery demonstration and a tray of pastries fell to the floor breaking a peach flan) I prayed, "Lord, show me from where I can get a baker's tray." Later the same day I was walking along the Evesham Road when a man came out of a shop with a baker's tray on his head. I knew the man (he had been a rodent operator, and had been to us to stop rats from the brook at the bottom of our garden). I said, "Oh! I could do with that tray to carry cakes to a party." "You can borrow it", he replied, "Just return it to the Town Hall when you have finished with it." God timed this encounter, though by then I had forgotten that I had earlier prayed for a tray. This was God's answer!

The Community Centre Hall was just round the corner from a maisonette we had bought for our daughter who had just become engaged. We thought the party could be a celebration for this, too, but the couple preferred it to be just for me. My sister took photographs that I looked at recently. The only regret at the time was that my parents were not alive to share the pleasure.

## Our Silver Wedding

We celebrated our silver wedding in September 1993 with a party at a local pub called "The Bell". Previously the caterers at the "Palace

Restaurant" in Redditch had looked after us very well. After that restaurant closed, the people who had run it became the proprietors of "The Bell". They said they would love to do a party meal for us there, which they did. All the guests said what a wonderful occasion it was. I wanted to give God thanks for all he had done for us in those 25 years, so I looked through my diaries to find some very interesting information. After the marvellous meal I gave a talk to our guests.

I spoke about God's numbers 3 and $7^{46}$. I received baptism by full immersion in 1967. We had our daughter in our third year of marriage, and we had three Guide Dogs following Kim who was there when we married. Afterwards Mitzie came, a black and tan Alsatian, next Honey, a small-boned sable Alsatian, and then Nicholas who was of mixed breed (Labrador, Retriever, and I suspect Poodle and Great Dane as he was large and curly coated).

We had been regularly attended 4 churches – Anglican, Baptist, Methodist and Pentecostal, and also 3 house churches. $^{(4+3=7)}$ We were members of 18 different organisations $^{(3 \ X \ 6)}$ and we had, between us, given talks to 322 gatherings of people. These included colleges, school children, Scouts and Guides and Brownies, and youth clubs; organisations such as the Soroptomists, The Business and Professional Women's Association, the Gas Federation, The Midlands Electricity Board; retirement groups such as Darby and Joan and the Sunset Over Sixty Group; Fellowships, Mothers' Union, Women's Institutes; clubs like Motorist Clubs, Inner Wheel, Rotary, Torch Fellowship, the British Legion, cricket clubs, Young Farmers Clubs and various Christian groups and guilds. Our names were circulated by word of mouth.

We had had 98 holidays $^{(7 \ X \ 14)}$ in 3 caravans in places ranging from eight to eighty miles away. Before we owned a caravan we had 7 holidays away together in Christian guest homes, hotels, and conference centres. We had stayed at Blackpool, Lee Abbey, Hildenborough Hall, Brunel Manor, West Watch, and Cloverley Hall and with the Barnabas Fellowship. Both Harold and I had the joy of visiting the Holy Land, though on separate occasions. My visit was

---

[46] See footnote 6

in 1966, before we married. For those who are interested I append my diary of the trip.

As for our "gift of hospitality", we had 133 people from 15 nations come to stay, or have a meal, or give talks, and all of them contributed to our visitors' book.

We bought or sold three houses and had 3 major lots of alterations (two extensions and a garage converted into a dining room and shower room at number 43).

The three of us (I first, then Abigail, then Harold) have all been in hospital for one problem or another, some serious, some not so serious. In these twenty-five years there had been 11 family weddings, and 20 funerals of friends and relations all attended by us. There had also been 14 births among close relatives.

We had owned 6 different cars of 3 makes – Allegros, Fiat and Subarus. (Since our 25$^{th}$ anniversary we have had another Subaru, in silver like the one for our silver wedding. I also had a silver one for my 73$^{rd}$ birthday when it represented "silver hairs among the gold"! The latest one is registered as R39 MDF (remembered by the mnemonic "Rejoice My Dear Friend").

## EPILOGUE

Although at the time of writing we are now living in the twenty-first century, my sister, who married in the twenty-first century, and is typing this for me, has suggested that I draw my account to a close on a note of celebration. After my spiritual rebirth at *Lee Abbey* I was called to a ministry of healing. God not only allowed me the privilege of serving him in this way, but he has provided for me and my husband throughout our lives in ways I have described. We have been able to witness to the love of God in sickness and in health, and we have known much happiness. We have been blessed in our families and in our many friends and acquaintances. Harold has had the pleasure of being accompanied by some wonderful guide dogs, and we have enjoyed motoring and caravanning together. We have seen the passing of loved ones and have joined in many celebrations. We have had many blessings, but we have also been sorely tested.

Harold has been tested by the loss of sight from boyhood, and we have both been tested by "The Old Devil". It would be impossible to recall the many times when we called upon God for his help and healing touch. Satan tries to sap one's faith by recurring situations where it seems that God is not listening and is a long way off. To see someone you love continue to suffer from blindness or eczema when you read in books, magazines, and letters, of others being healed is very hard. I was reminded that

> "He who would advance in grace, who would Christ's image wear,
> Must oft behold his smiling face, in humble, pleading prayer."[47]

I am very glad that I took the advice of Leslie Sutton to keep a journal. It is so easy to forget what God has done in the past. He wants future generations to know Who He is and what he has done. He also wants them to know how to live so that, in keeping his commandments, goodness and mercy may follow them all the days of their lives. May Jesus Christ be praised in all thing.

---

[47] Translated from the French of Jeanne Guyon by Thomas Upham (1799-1872) "A Method of Prayer"

# APPENDIX:
## THE HOLY LAND TOUR

I had been to a slide show on the Holy Land given by a Catholic Minister who had lived there several years as a missionary. This had whetted my appetite to go there and see it all for myself. I had put it to the Lord in prayer and the answer he had given was to go to all Samaria and Judea, so I made preparations by having all the injections needed for such a trip in March. Then I learnt that the Guild of Health was organising a tour later in the year, in May, to be led by Canon Wallace Bird who had spoken two months before to a Guild of Health conference on *Divine Healing*. The cost of the holiday was £118.

May came, and our flight out to Amman was uneventful. We were driven to Jerusalem by taxi from Amman, but it was in the very early hours and pitch dark, so we saw little of the journey, travelling from 1.00 a.m. until we got into our beds in Jerusalem at 4.00 a.m. We had four hours' sleep before getting up for breakfast and **our first day** tour.

**Day 1**

This day took us to the village of Bethany where we saw the tomb of Lazarus, the chapel and garden. We read the story from St. John's Gospel[48] before we walked up the hill to Bethphage, and to the shrine on the Mount of Olives where Jesus obtained the ass on which he rode into Jerusalem. We walked the same road, overlooking the Kidron Valley, mingling with the ordinary folk, children and animals until we reached the Chapel of the Ascension at the top of the Mount of Olives, where, the story goes, Christ left his footprint in the rock as he left the earth. There was a footprint there, but I did not feel it to be one of our Lord's. From here we descended the stony pathway to the Garden of Gethsemane. It was so much smaller than I had imagined, but the old olive grove still seemed to hold the sacredness of the spot. Over the rock of agony the Church of All Nations had been built in which all nations and denominations could hold services. We arrived when most other tourists were departing, so we held our own service there and all forty-four of our party felt greatly moved. This was an unforgettable memory. Looking from the

---

[48] John 11: 1-43

garden back to Jerusalem, we saw the Golden Gate through which the soldiers came to capture Jesus. In the valley by the garden our taxi collected us and took us back to our hotel for lunch. In the afternoon we rested and had a talk from our leader.

**Day 2**

The second day's tour found us going to Bethlehem, seeing Rachel's tomb on the way. We visited the Church of the Nativity, where we sang "O Come All Ye Faithful", the Chapel of the Innocents, St. Jerome's tomb, the Crusaders' tomb and the entrance to St. Catherine's Church. Then we went on to the Shepherds' Fields where we were glad to sit in the cool of a small cave and sing "While Shepherds watched their Flocks by Night". It seemed strange to sing this in May, in the heat of the day, and so far from Christmas Day, yet we felt very close to the birth of Jesus. Some wished to go on to Hebron where we saw Abraham's tomb and the tombs of Isaac, Sarah, Jacob, Rebekah, and Joseph. We had no guide with us, but we saw people being given what looked like chicken legs to eat in the mosque. Then we went back to Jerusalem and saw St. Stephen's Gate, the cave of Mary's birth, St. Anne's Church and well, and the pool of Bethesda, which was nothing like I had visualised it from artists' paintings and drawings. It was rather dark, dismal, and barren, and not at all inviting. Then we went on to the ruins of old Jerusalem, up King Feisal Street to the Dome of the Rock, the Temple area, King Solomon's Temple, the Wailing Wall, King Herod's Temple and so on, all of which had their meaning in history.

**Day 3**

On the third day we took the road to Damascus, seeing on the way Bedouin tents and camp site. The Jordan River, the Jordanian hills, Wilderness Mountains, orange groves, lemon groves, grape vines and tomatoes, were all seen on the way. We passed a Gypsy cavalcade and encampment. The gypsies were all on donkeys, a very rare sight, and I was able to capture them on my camera through the windscreen of the car as we moved along. Also of interest were the camels and goats and the wild flowers, poppies and flax, wheat and barley. There were small village schools where, I was told, children start at age 7 and leave at 12. In passing we saw the River Jabok and Roman caves and tombs. Mount Hermon was

176

snow-covered, and, since it was a watershed, there was a vast cultivated expanse round it and forestry trees, sheep and goats.

We stopped at Derra to fill up with petrol. There, on the roadside, were stalls selling eggs, pigeons and doves. We saw our first train, and then passed through more villages with flat-roofed mud and stone houses, then miles of flat land, with orchards of apricots, almonds and olives.

We arrived finally at Damascus at 12.15 p.m. for lunch. Then we entered the coach to be taken round the city. We saw the "Street called Straight"[49], the East and West Gate, the window from which St. Paul was let down in a basket, the house of Ananias, and the Palace where we saw the mother-of-pearl room, the glass room, and the cabinet and bathing rooms.

Down one street we saw shops of craft workers – wood carving, skin curing, shoe making and basket making. It was very interesting to see them all in one street.

Another place of interest to which we were taken was Beeroth, where Mary and Joseph realised the boy Jesus was missing from the party and returned to Jerusalem, where they found him in the Temple. The surrounding land was barren, with terraces on the rocks, but few trees. Beeroth has plenty of water and is a summer resort. It is 375 feet higher than Jerusalem, according to our guide. Bethel was another place we saw. The name Bethel means house of God. It was where Jacob saw in his dream a ladder stretching up to heaven, and the place where tithing began.

We travelled on through a fertile valley on a road with hairpin bends that had been built by the Turks 400 years earlier. Shiloh, meaning place of rest, is a city of Ephraim surrounded by barren mountains where we passed a military hospital.

After leaving Jerusalem for Samaria we stopped to view the land – fertile plain with small plots of land and rocky, barren, hills round it. King Omri's palace has views that stretch to the Mediterranean Sea, and to Galilee and Nazareth. A garden has been built surrounding Jacob's Well, with beautiful hibiscus and jacaranda trees, palms, and lemon and orange trees. It was lovely to sit in an oasis of beauty waiting our turn to visit the well. We were handed a cup of cool,

[49] Acts: 9: 11

177

refreshing, water from the well which is 172 feet deep. It took 3 seconds for a drop of water tipped back into the well to be heard splashing into the water. Seen from the well is Mount Gerizim, where, according to the book of Judges, Jothan spoke to the men of Shechem[50].

We went to see the remains of a thirteenth century amphitheatre of Greek origin that was crumbling in parts, but still recognisable as an amphitheatre. We got back into our taxis which, I learnt, were American Plymouths and then cost £3,300 to £4,000. They were very comfortable. We drove through some fertile land and passed by farms, almond trees, a Roman aqueduct, a leper hospital, and a soup factory, and so back to our hotel for lunch.

In the afternoon our party walked the way of the cross, stopping for prayer and readings at all of the fourteen stations along the Via Dolorosa. This was very moving in spite of the noise and bustle that went on around our walk of silence and meditation.

We then saw the Church of the Holy Sepulchre where a service was in progress. We waited in a queue of tourists some of whom were acting very irreverently. I heard the words of Jesus, "Father, forgive them, for they know not what they do."[51] We took our turn to file past the two stations where Mary received Jesus, and the crucifixion spot, and where the earthquake caused a crack in the rock, down to the tomb of Joseph of Arimathea which we entered. Then we went to another section of the Church where an Armenian service was being sung and to the Catholic part where the stone on which Christ was flailed was shown to us. A short service was held for us before we returned to our hotel. We all reflected on what we had just seen and done. To me a heavy weight of worldliness and sin was still evident, the divided Church showing the division of the church today. It seemed so artificial in the noise and press and throng of tourists, for whom it was just another thing seen and done, since they did not know Jesus or the cost to him of enabling them to know God and heaven. The lack of reverence and respect must have hurt the heart of the Lord.

---

[50] Judges 9: 7-21
[51] Luke 23: 34

**Day 4**

The fourth morning saw us visiting the Church of St. Peter Gallicantu, a church in three tiers on the supposed site of the House of Caiaphas. It is where the Lord turned and looked upon Peter after he had denied him three times. Below is a 4<sup>th</sup> Century prison pit from which you can look up through a grille to the altar above. I said, out loud, "I've seen all this before in a dream I had while I was at boarding school. It was identical in every way. I had, until then, thought the dream was due to my doing a study of churches in Italy. I had thought no more about it until given the revelation that it was St. Peter's Jerusalem, not St. Peter's Rome. It was deeply moving to see the authentic cells; the signs and pictures on the wall of a crucifix; the prisoners' flailing yard and the rest chairs there, with holes for tying hands and feet. St. John and St. Peter were flagellated there, but not Christ. There were holes for water used to wash wounds, for vinegar for deadening pain, and for ropes and chains to pass over the rock seats. Guards watched prisoners from special sentry posts, with seats which had special indents for their feet carved out of stone to make the seats more comfortable. I felt here the reality of the building; and the horrors of its past left a heaviness and chill that touched my soul and spirit. I was glad to leave for another tour in the afternoon to Jericho and the Dead Sea and Qumran. Jericho, we were told, is 800 feet below sea level and it is also the oldest city in the world. There were 10,500 refugees living in the outskirts. We were taken to see parts of the city wall that had fallen down in the battle of Jericho in Bible times, when Joshua led his men round the walls shouting and blowing trumpets, as God had commanded, so as to gain entrance to the city. Round about are the salt mountains where the water in the Jordan valley had dried out.

We visited the river Jordan at the place where Jesus was baptised by John the Baptist, and here we entered an open rowing boat to row a few yards up and down river. From this place you could look and see only dry, arid, rock, except for a few trees planted by the water side. In the far distance were the hills and the mountains of the wilderness where Christ fasted for forty days. The river Jordan, 1,000 feet below sea level, was not as big as I had imagined, but we were glad of an oasis of trees nearby where we could sit and rest and pray and refresh ourselves before further travel to the caves at

179

Qumran where the shepherd boy found the scrolls. We saw them later in a museum. The air was perfectly clear, as there was no pollution from factories or city waste. The shimmering of the air from the heat, the golden glow of the rocks in the foreground, and the blue of the sea, and pink of the hills beyond, made a perfect setting for meditation. It was far from crowds, telephones and cars. There was not even a bird to sing in the air. It was all but dead, until our guide suddenly stopped the car and dashed towards a little group of people. He had spotted a poisonous snake, but was able to deal with it and protect us from harm. We called back at a hotel by the Dead Sea to pick up a few people who had wanted to go swimming in the sea instead of visiting the caves of Qumran. There was so much to photograph that I was glad to have taken my camera.

**Day 5**

On the fifth day we were on the road to Emmaus, where we visited and entered a church and garden to commemorate the place where our Lord walked with his disciples after his resurrection, but they did not recognise him until he broke bread in their home. On our return we were taken to the Mount of Olives where we had a sundown service together at the top, and walked back down to Jerusalem to our hotel. That night I was invited by our guide to go with him to see a cabaret at a hotel, and then to be driven around the city, and on to a village to take a friend to his home. On the way back we had to get the keys from the gate keeper to re-enter the city just after midnight. I thought of the hymn verse, "He only could unlock the gate of Heaven and let us in". I was glad that our group were covering us in prayer all the time. I was able to witness to the guide whilst seeing the twinkling lights of the city from the surrounding hills. This gave me another experience to remember all my life.

**Day 6**

On the sixth day we visited the Helen Keller home of the Bible Lands Society. It had started with 4 girls in a flat. Now people 18 years and upwards worked at transcribing Braille and making handicrafts which we could purchase. Then it cost £5 per week per student and, under an adoption scheme, £26 kept one person in food and clothing for a year. Mother-of pearl and olive wood goods were sent to a shop in London, as were pottery, basketry, woven and knitted goods, rugs, "pull-through" type, bags and serviettes. We saw these articles being made and also the finished products. There was a clay model of the garden. Students felt the model to learn the layout of the garden.

In the afternoon we visited a Leper Hospital where we saw a man without arms, legs, or sight, but who had been cured of the disease. In 1947 drugs became available but it could take 4 years to become free of the disease. The gardens were beautifully laid out and, as I had begun to feel faint indoors, I walked about photographing the flowers. I missed the evening tour to the Ecce Homo Orphanage, but walked instead up St. Mark's Road where Jesus walked when he left the Upper Room for Gethsemane.

**Day 7**

We changed over to the Israeli side and visited Mount Zion, King David's Tomb, the museum where we saw the Dead Sea Scrolls, the Church of the Assumption of the Blessed Virgin Mary, and then the Benedictine Abbey. The thing that struck me most was the Mount Zion Memorial to all dead Jews from the 1939-45 war.

We were given lunch at the YMCA. After boarding a coach for the rest of our pilgrimage we passed through a valley full of apple orchards, with terraced slopes and modern flats and other buildings. These were a complete contrast from what we had seen on the Jordanian side of the Mandelbaum Gate. We learnt that a forest of pine trees we saw had been planted by the British. On the road side were disused tanks – a memorial of the 1947 war. We passed on through Sampson's country, where we saw a corn harvest, vineyards, and sugar beet, all well watered by irrigation sprays. There we had our first sight of an electric train. We went through Lod, past an airport, and on to an orange packing station where 50,000 cases of Jaffa oranges were packed and sent to Europe every year. Nearby was a lemon grove, enclosed by cypress trees. There was also a nursery for trees, roses, cactus hedges, mimosa, and palm trees. I noticed there were few petrol filling stations. As we drove along we saw farms, mostly small holdings, bananas, tomatoes, and sugar beet. We went through an empty Arab village and back into hills and stony country.

We arrived at our destination, the City of Tiberias, hot, tired, and hungry. These discomforts were soon remedied, and the view from the hospice was marvellous, across the Sea of Galilee with the Golan

Heights in the distance on the far side of the Sea. We celebrated Holy Communion on the front lawn of the hospice at 7.15 a.m. before breakfast at 7.45 a.m. I took photographs of bougainvillaea and jacaranda trees and palms. They made a frame for the blue sea. A yacht with a red sail came into view just beyond the garden. What a back-cloth for an Altar table!

**Day 8**

On the 8th Day we visited Nazareth and went to the well where the Holy Family drew their water, and to the home where they lived. It was like a rock cavern house – so cool and refreshing! We wanted to rest a while before going up the hill to visit the hospital which had 300 beds, 45 doctors and trainee doctors, and 140 nurses. We had a tour round the maternity wards and had a service in the hospital chapel. It was all very interesting. On the way back we saw Mount Tabor and, in the distance, the village of Cain which we were able to visit later. In the valley of Jezreel were vast acres of cultivated land, but no sign of any farm buildings, though there is a sugar beet factory in Afula. Jews from all over the world had returned to begin a new life in their land, and it was obvious that they were very industrious to make the land plentiful again. Mount Tabor being 1,930 feet high, and the Sea of Galilee 7,000 feet below sea level, we had a down-hill run all the way back. Our bus driver, a German Jew, had done two and a half years of military training from the age of 18 and had to return for further training for 10 hours a month. He was both a bus driver and an officer in the army.

**Day 9**

On Day 9 we went to the Dome church on the Mount of the Beatitudes where we had a service. It is a most beautiful place, overlooking the Sea of Galilee. The hill sides, and slopes all round the Sea, looked to me just like views in the English Lake District. We had a short stop at Magdala, where Mary Magdalene was born, and at Tagbatha, where we saw the floor covered with mosaics to commemorate the spot where Jesus met Peter and told him to follow him. We also passed the spot where Jesus made breakfast on the shore for his disciples. Over the entrance was a plaque saying, "Simon Peter, lovest thou me? Feed my sheep."[52]

We visited Capernaum to see the remains of the synagogue built by the centurion whose servant was healed by Jesus. We sat and rested in the shade by the shore where we waited for the boat to take us across the Sea of Galilee. While we waited the guide gave us some details about the Sea. It is 13 miles long and 7 miles wide and 116 feet deep. Its water comes from the Jordan, from rainwater and from springs. It flows out to the river Jordan and on to the Dead Sea. Fishing is done at night and there are 32 different kinds of fish. In rough, windy, weather the waves can be whipped up to 7 metres high.

We crossed over to a Kibbutz where 2,500 people lived in 280 communities. They lived on bananas, water melons, dates, grapes, olives, chickens and fish. As there was no private money, each person helped the others and a budget was made for all. Funds were received from America. They ran a fish canning factory and had ponds to stock up the fish. They also ran a boat company, a restaurant, and a camp for campers. It was a demilitarised zone and their hard work was repaid. They worked for peace not war.

We were entertained to lunch at a Kibbutz. A meal of Saint Peter's fish, straight from the sea, was delicious. We looked round the Kibbutz and then swam in the lovely, clear, water which was warm like a bath at the shallow edge where stones reflected the sun's heat.

Our coach met us and took us back by road along the Jordan valley, past banana groves, a chicken farm, and a honey farm. In the evening there was a gathering in the hospice where all members shared their feelings about the trip, their experiences of God speaking to them. One lady recited a poem on Jesus of Nazareth as a carpenter, which I enjoyed so much that I took down a copy to keep.

At night I went with the guide to see the Israeli National Dancers at a lakeside resort hotel. It was a special privilege as it was difficult to obtain tickets as the group was popular. They were very good.

---

[52] John 21:17

**Day 10**

We arose early to have another long trip to Acre, Haifa, and Caesarea Philippi. We had lunch at a mental hospital where we were allowed to talk to the patients who had come from all over the globe. At Caesarea we were taken to an amphitheatre built by Herod and restored and used at that time. We sang psalms and hymns there, looking out to the sea which formed a backcloth to the stage. Acre had old ruins in the harbour area which dated back to the wars of the crusaders. It was incongruous to see the new mixing with the old – TV aerials and washing hung out on the roof tops. Haifa was beautiful, seen from the hill top that overlooked both it and the Mediterranean Sea. There were big grain ships in dock, loading and unloading their cargoes. On the trip we saw crops of maize, grapefruit, and olives, but the only birds seen were a large buzzard, an owl, and a linnet.

**Day 11**

We were up at 2.45 a.m. to leave at 3.30 a.m. by mini bus for a sunrise service on Mount Tabor. It was so warm we were only in cotton dresses and cardigans even at that hour. We looked out over the cultivated land and saw cloud layers from the valley, and a mackerel sky was the backcloth to a wrought iron cross. The party sat together for the service of breaking of bread. We were near the Russian Orthodox Church of the Transfiguration. It was locked at that hour, but we later saw slides and postcards of its interior in a shop. After the service we walked back down to the mini bus to get back to the hospice for 8.00 a.m. breakfast. The rest of the day was free, so I took my camera and wandered round the lakeside photographing the harbour and people fishing and water-skiing. By 11.00 a.m. the heat had increased so much I went back to the hospice until 4.00 p.m., when I went out up the lakeside in the other direction to see wild flowers – hollyhocks, poppies, cyclamen, cornflowers, anemones, oleanders etc.

**Day 12**

This was a Sunday. I was up at 5.00 a.m. to see the most beautiful sunrise over Galilee, with rays from the sun to the sea, and fishermen in their boats. Exquisite! So I hurriedly dressed, got my camera, took pictures from the balcony, and went out into the garden. I went

184

down to the town and saw fishermen selling their catch, boxes of fish, and I followed them on carts and up to the shops. I was back in time for 8.00 a.m. breakfast. At 9.45 a.m. the whole party left for a service together on the hillside by the lake, but there was much discomfort from the heat, flies, thorns, sand and stony ground and from weariness. We all shared what the pilgrimage had meant to us, what we felt about the holiday spiritually, mentally, and physically, and how we could make use of the trip when we returned. Sixteen years later I was still showing my slides and giving talks on the Holy Land. In the evening we attended the Scottish Church in Tiberias for evensong.

**Day 13**

We stopped at the village of Nain and went to the chapel where we sang hymns and psalms which attracted the villagers. As it was the last stop before we arrived at the airport at Tel Aviv, we gave our small coins to the children. What joy and delight showed in their faces! At the airport we had a five-course meal and then found we had a four hour delay. We took off at 5.55 p.m. and arrived in London at 11.55 p.m. and got to bed at 1.15 a.m. on Day 14. We stayed in London for the night before catching the Pullman to Birmingham. I was home at 1.15 p.m.

# INDEX

Lightning Source UK Ltd.
Milton Keynes UK
24 January 2011

166307UK00002B/35/P

9 781449 049843